AN OCTAGON FOR THE CURRIERS

An Octagon for the Curriers

by Melanie Meyers and Frank Angelo

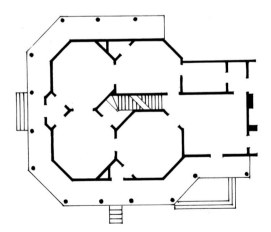

PUBLISHED BY
FREDERICK P. CURRIER, POST PUBLISHING

210 Post Street, Suite 903
San Francisco, CA 94108

Library of Congress Cataloging-in-Publication Number: 95-069824

ISBN: 0-9645916-0-X

Book design by Robin Weiss Graphic Design.
The typeface is Century Schoolbook.
Typography and composition by Robin Weiss Graphic Design.

This book was printed by Global Interprint, Petaluma.
Creative direction provided by Frederick P. Currier and Tara T. Cacciola.
Production was limited to 2,000 copies.

Post Publishing
210 Post Street, Suite 903
San Francisco, CA 94108

Printed in Hong Kong.

CONTENTS

LOWER CANADA

Copper Mine

St Marys R.

St Mary's Str. & Falls
Str of Michilimacinack
St Josephs I.
L. Nipissing

Uttawas R.

Green Bay

Mine

Ottawas & Miamies

G. Traverse B.

Gloucester B.

Montreal

Sorell R.

Sincoe L

Six Nations

Kingston

Champlain

Plattsburg

Ogdensburg

Lake Champlain

MICHIGAN

TORONTO

London

LAKE ONTARIO
100 m.

Black R.
Watertown
Whitehall
Sackets Harbour
L. George
Rome
Utica
Saratoga

Saginaw
Ft Gratiot
Palmer
Byron
Grand R.

St Clair
Thames R.
Niagara Falls
Grand L.
Lockpt.
Erie Canal
363

Rochester
Geneva
Auburn
Mohawk R.150
ALBANY
Troy

DETROIT
Detroit R.
St Clair

Buffalo

NEW
Ithaca
YORK

Browns T.
French T.

LAKE ERIE
270 m.

Erie
Dunk.

Binghamton

Hudson

Catskill

chicago

S. Josephs R.

Maumee R.

Cleveland
Sandusky
Canal

Meadville

Meansville

West Br.

Williamsport

Poughkeepsie

Newburg

West Pt

Potawatomie Indians

R. 400

Fort Wayne

Sandusky River
Wooster

PENNSYLVANIA
Northumberland
Wilkesbarre
Reading
Patterson

N York

Newark

Wabash R. 500

Stubenville

Pittsburg

Huntington

Carlisle

N. Brunswick

INDIANA

OHIO

Newark

Wheeling
Chambersburg

HARRISBURG
Lancaster

White R.

Jacksonboro

INDIANAPOLIS

COLUMBUS

Zanesville

York

Philadelphia

TRENTON

Dayton
Circleville

Hagers T.
Frederick T.

Baltimore

Wilmington

N. Castle

Columbus
Chillicothe
Marietta

Winchester

MARYLAND

DOVER

Vevay

Cincinnati

L. Kanhawa R.

ANNAPOLIS

Vincennes

Newport

Portsmouth

Shenandoah

WASHINGTON

N. Albany
Louisville
Maysville

FRANKFORT

Charleston
Stanton

Fredericksburg

Rappahannock R.

Harmony
Rockport
Versailles
Lexington

Lexington

Charlottesville

FOREWORD

On a quiet side street in the rural Michigan hamlet of Almont stands a house whose history is, in so many ways, a microcosm of the history of Michigan itself.

At the most basic level, the Currier Octagon house was a home for a pioneering Michigan family and its patriarch, Frederick Plumer Currier. Currier was one of thousands of New Englanders who were attracted to the open and fertile land of Michigan in the decades after the end of the War of 1812. Those Yankees flooded into Michigan, swelling its population from a mere 30,000 in 1830 to nearly 220,000 ten years later. In the process, they transformed Michigan into an extension of New England. More than any other state in the American west of the mid-nineteenth century, Michigan exhibited distinctive Yankee characteristics. The transplanted New Englanders adopted the traditions of their forebears, writing into Michigan's state

1. 19th century map, 1835
This 1835 map shows the ease by which Frederick Plumer Currier I could travel from mid-state Vermont on the Connecticut River, via the Erie Canal, to Buffalo then to Detroit; it was a trip he made often after 1840.

constitution provisions for the public support of education. Later state legislatures abolished capital punishment, took steps to wipe out liquor, and gave support to their constituents' efforts to aid and abet the destruction of the slave system of the cotton South.

They also planted strong economic and financial roots, and in this context the life story of the first Frederick Currier becomes symbolic of larger trends. He was willing to speculate, invest, fail and try again, consistently resilient, always optimistic, reflecting well his America of the mid-nineteenth century. That period in our country's history was one during which the nation looked inward, no longer relying on Europe for inspiration in its art, literature, history, and architecture. In the heady decades of the 1830s and 1840s, Americans became more consciously American. Out of this new sense of nationhood came a full flowering of change, as artists looked to the land around them for inspiration and writers cast their stories in distinctly American settings and on uniquely American themes. As the generation that had led the nation through its eras of colonization and revolution passed from the scene, a new generation arose whose birthright was American not European, free not colonial. To them, the stories of the American Revolution were found in history books not in their own recollections; their destiny then was to cast off the trappings of the old world and take on the mantle of the new.

This movement was evident especially in architecture. The traditions of colonial and Georgian designs were perceived as passé and harkening back to a completely different generation. Distinctly American ideas were what excited these new Americans, and Orson Fowler had a head full of ideas. His octagon style designs captured the mood of the time and the imagination of many, including Frederick Currier. Applying his craftsman's skills, the elder Currier fashioned a home in his adopted town of Almont, Michigan, that embodied outside as well as inside the essence of Fowler's philosophy. When it was completed and his family settled into it, Currier's octagon became a single, but nonetheless crucially important, physical manifestation of two threads of Jacksonian America, the hardy pioneer and a conspicuously strong sense of national identity.

There is more to this book, however, than the intertwined stories of a man and his house. There is also the story of Almont, Michigan, itself, and the changes it has undergone since its founding in the 1830s. Its name itself reflects the time of its settlement, honoring as it does a Mexican hero in his country's battle against Texas independence. Why would residents of a rural Michigan farming community be interested in affairs more than a thousand miles away? As was true of many Northerners, Michiganians viewed with concern the prospects a Texas victory in the Mexican War would have for the future expansion of slavery beyond the cotton South. Although many Northerners might begrudgingly tolerate slavery in what was argued as its natural environment the deep South, they were deeply concerned over the threat of the expansion of slavery into the great trans-Mississippi west. The Mexican War was the first of many signs to Northerners that they might have to take drastic action in the future to head off the push of slavery into unsettled lands. For the moment, residents of Bristol could at least register their alarm by renaming their village Almont in recognition of Juan Almonte, the Mexican minister to the United States, who officially broke off diplomatic relations with this country when U.S. President James K. Polk signed the Texas bill of independence into law in 1845.

To many contemporary residents of Almont that story has probably been relegated to the back reaches of quaint local history, as the town is now being drawn closer and closer into the ever-growing orbit of the expanding Detroit metropolis. Through all those many changes, the Currier Octagon has remained, not unchanged of course, but essentially what it always was, a uniquely historic home. But not always a home for the Curriers, as it turned out. And that brings into the story the fourth Frederick P. Currier. It was he who bought the house in 1985, bringing it back into Currier family ownership and then took the next important step, an investment in its restoration. Recognizing that a sturdy foundation, good construction techniques, and sympathetic ownership can only help, to a degree, a structure survive the ravages of time and weather, Frederick P. Currier IV spent his own money to ensure that the Currier Octagon will stand into Michigan's twenty first century as a physical reminder of its nineteenth century.

And, finally, the story of the Currier Octagon includes reference to one Lewis Fitch, a close family friend whose photographic abilities provided opportunities for him to remain in contact with the apparent love of his life, Sarah Currier Owens. Fitch's work was not merely a labor of love, however, for he had an eye for setting, framing, and balance that elevated his work to art, beyond the simple needs to capture a moment on film. And, here again, the role of Frederick P. Currier IV becomes important, for he has insisted that the photography of Lewis Fitch deserves special attention, not simply as illustrative embellishments in this book, but in a publication devoted to the full corpus of Fitch's photographic work. That will be the subject of a companion volume to this one, and will complete the process of intertwining that began when an intrepid, 42-year old transplanted New Englander supervised the laying of the oak foundations for his new home on the Michigan frontier.

Thomas L. Jones
Ypsilanti, Michigan

PREFACE

When I first decided to do a book on the octagon house my great grandfather, Frederick P. Currier I, built in Almont, Michigan in 1854, I thought, like many other first time authors, that it would be a simple matter.

It turned out just the opposite, which should come to no surprise to those who have taken on a similar task.

The basic issue I faced, of course, was the focus of the book; the reader will find here a multi faceted story. There is information about the house itself and my great grandfather and his offspring. There are also details regarding the town of Almont, Michigan. Throughout the book are some wonderful turn of the century photographs taken by Lewis Fitch, a close friend of the Currier family.

The reader will come to know my great grandfather through this book or at least as much as could be gleaned about him from public records, family stories,

---

2. Frederick P. Currier, about 1865
This cabinet card is the earliest known image of FPC I and was taken when he was 53 years old.

and much deduction. It is clear that Frederick P. Currier I was a taciturn, tall, thin New Englander. He had a tremendous amount of drive as seen in his long and varied business career. He influenced his two brothers, Moses and Richard, to leave their native Vermont which they all loved and join him in Michigan. He set down deep family and financial roots in Michigan, yet he regularly made it a practice to go back to New England via the water route provided by the Erie Canal to return to Newbury, Vermont, and the general area of the Connecticut River. Despite the rigors of nineteenth century travel, he was committed to keeping in personal touch with his New England origins.

In truth, it was much easier to analyze the house my great grandfather built than to discover accurately the person he was, and that is because the house he lovingly designed and constructed one hundred and forty years ago still stands. Clearly, Frederick P. Currier I was influenced by the mid-nineteenth century promoter of octagon style architecture, Orson Fowler, and combined Fowler's concept and his own ability as a builder to make his home unique both on the exterior and in the interior. Its symmetry is still beautiful after nearly a century and a half. The story of the house also would not have been complete without telling about my own decision to purchase and restore it. That is the subject of the final chapter.

This book is the product of good advice and counsel from Frank Angelo, an editor friend from my days at the Detroit Free Press. It was Frank who suggested that its central focus be the house as a unique symbol intertwining the lives of four generations of Curriers. The heart of the narrative is the work of Melanie Meyers, whose research into the history of Almont, Orson Fowler, and my family forms the basis on which the total project rests. To both Frank and Melanie I express my profound thanks for jobs well done.

There are at least three or four more people who gave of their time and energy to this project during the many years of gestation, among them Thomas Halsted, one of the country's finest photographic dealers. He sorted through all the Fitch images taken around Almont and Yale and gave us his professional opinion about the ones that really stood out.

In addition, Robert "Shell" Hensleigh, one of the Detroit Institute of Art's fine professionals, is responsible for all of the photographic copy work and many wonderful exterior and interior shots. With his expertise in the darkroom he was able to print images as close to the original intent of the photographer as possible. He spent a lot of time above and beyond the call of the dollar.

Tara T. Cacciola, who came into the project late, with her enthusiasm, drive and careful work helped to make this book a level above the ordinary.

Robin Weiss, the designer, has helped immeasurably to bring this project to a quality level which we all can admire.

And of course, last and not least I have to mention Philip Currier, of Henniker, New Hampshire, the country's leading genealogist of all Curriers in the United States. My children Nancy, Amelia and Rebecca; my brother Dr. Robert Currier; my sister Sue Shaker, and of course my very supportive wife Amy McCombs all helped fan the flame when it appeared water logged by one thing or another.

A long and slow walk through the mists of history in my family seems to give me a better understanding of who I am. Remembrances of my grandfather, tall and quiet, handing me as a young person, pink and white peppermints and sitting upright in his chair, will always be in my memory. I have strong memories of my aunt Mayme who became the family repository of the many interesting anecdotes about Sarah Currier, Henry Currier, and her grandfather Frederick P. Currier I. The three pillars in her life were the Congregational Church, the Detroit Tigers, and the Republican Party. These, along with her sharp sense of humor, combined to create a truly spirited woman who was always the most sympathetic listener to the woes of my brother and I during our many visits to either cut her lawn or just talk.

My visits to the Currier Octagon always provide me with greater and greater admiration of its interior design and flow, formed by four octagon rooms on the first floor and four similarly designed chambers on the second floor, the cut-in stairway, the full windows down to the floor, and the fine quality of the molding and all the interior woodwork. I also marvel at the structure's longevity, especially considering its timbered foundation and wooden exterior. It stands as a testimony to those who designed and built it and those who called it home since the 1850s.

Some of the house's original exterior detailing has been lost over the years. Eventually, wrought-iron fencing and decorative iron work around the top roof and the second floor roof will be added for historical accuracy. The asphalt shingles, however, will undoubtedly remain; they replaced the original cedar shingles years ago.

Woven into the narrative are stories about the Currier family, but preparing this aspect of the book created some problems because more information has come down to me through the family about the Frederick and Moses lines than the Richard Currier line. Nevertheless, contemporary Curriers will presumably find enough family history to be satisfied with the effort.

One final word about Lewis Fitch, whose photographs enhance this book. He was an interesting character in his own right, and his story added so much to that of the Curriers and their octagon. Fitch was apparently quite in love with my great aunt Sarah. That she was married meant that his affection was platonic; it was sincere and long-lived, however. Fitch had been a member of the Fifth Cavalry during the Civil War and fought under George Armstrong Custer in numerous campaigns. Discharged at Fort Leavenworth, Kansas, Fitch returned to Yale, Michigan and became a well respected and successful jeweler. His jewelry skills were applied with stunning results to the art of photography. His eye captured the totality of life around him, the factories, the people, the families, the horses, the main streets. He often put his photographs into books and gave them as presents during the holidays. My great aunt Sarah kept those photographic books and they have remained a cherished treasure in the Currier family.

Fitch loved the quiet, bucolic life of rural Michigan probably because it contrasted so sharply to the chaos and noise of his war experiences. Some of Fitch's work is in this book, but, in truth, he deserves special attention. A book of his photographs and his life is in preparation and will be published at a later date as a companion to this volume.

Frederick P. Currier IV
San Francisco, California.

ACKNOWLEDGMENTS

Frederick Currier first and foremost, whose ideas and dedication gave birth to this project, and for his continued encouragement and belief in my abilities.

Currier family members for sharing their family history.

Thomas Jones, former executive director of the Historical Society of Michigan, for his enthusiasm for history, administrative suggestions and for recommending me for this project.

Marshall McLennan, director of Eastern Michigan University's Historic Preservation Program, for his continued support and assistance with historic context and thorough editing.

Robert Schweitzer, historic preservation consultant and author, for sharing his knowledge of Michigan octagons and Orson Fowler.

Robert Christensen, Michigan Bureau of History, for sharing his extensive knowledge of Michigan's built environment.

Kay Torney, head librarian of Henry L. Stephens Library in Almont, Michigan, for her assistance in primary research and extensive knowledge in local history.

Jeffery F. Winstel, planner and historian, AICP, for sharing his ideas and enthusiasm for this project and attention to detail in producing accurate floor plans.

Alanna Lee Meyers for her undying patience in nursing me through my severe back injury during this project.

Rhona Lisa Meyers, freelance writer and editor, for helpful editing suggestions.

And the citizens of Almont , for their help with local history, general assistance and good food.

Melanie A. Meyers
Cleveland, Ohio

This book is dedicated to all who are Curriers, whether by blood or marriage, and to all who love the unique Octagon houses.

Res. of F.P. Currier, Esq. Almont

CHAPTER ONE

A New Englander moves to Michigan in 1842

For Frederick Plumer Currier the timing of his arrival in Michigan was perfect. Michigan had achieved statehood in 1837. Its forests were beginning to yield the hardwoods that helped build the Chicagos and Cincinnatis of the country. Opportunity beckoned for hundreds of newcomers.

Currier arrived in 1842, returned briefly to the home he had left in New England, and then settled permanently in Michigan in 1846. He was an authentic Michigan pioneer who brought with him unbounded enthusiasm, the restless spirit of an entrepreneur, and a set of values honed in a stern New England religious tradition.

By the time of his death in 1900, he had helped to build a community—Almont—and, with his family, left an indelible mark on Michigan's Thumb area heritage. From a historical perspective it also is appropriate that the many-faceted Currier should leave a

---

3. Engraving, 1870's
Done in the 1870's, this lithograph is the earliest recorded image of the Currier Octagon. The decorative grill work on the roof and edges of the second and third floors is faithfully recorded by the artist, along with the detailed fence, windows and doors.

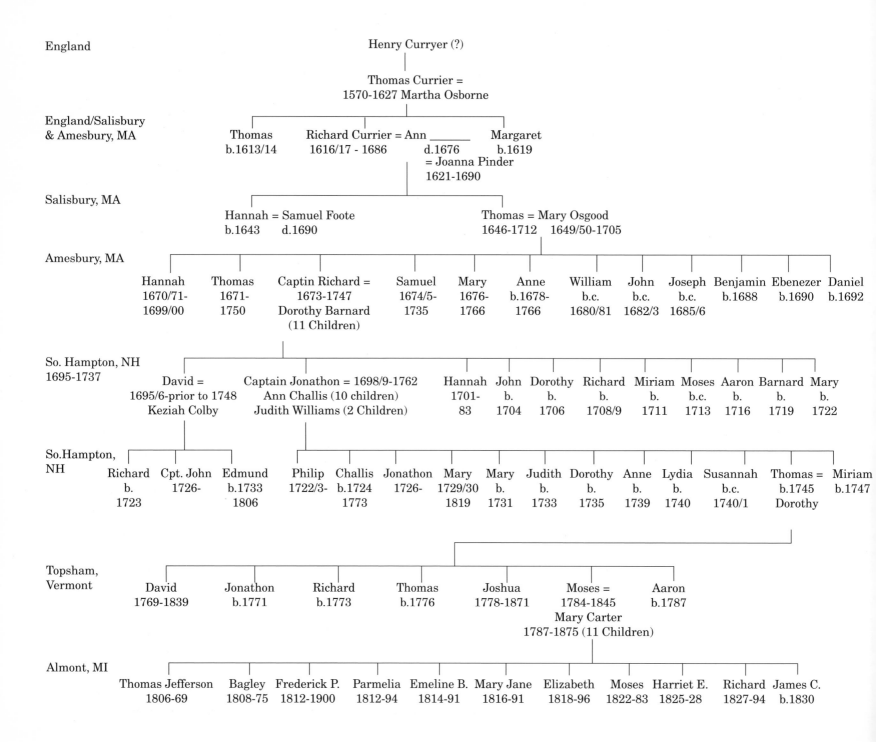

England

Henry Curryer (?)

Thomas Currier =
1570-1627 Martha Osborne

England/Salisbury
& Amesbury, MA

Thomas
b.1613/14

Richard Currier = Ann _____
1616/17 - 1686   d.1676
= Joanna Pinder
1621-1690

Margaret
b.1619

Salisbury, MA

Hannah = Samuel Foote
b.1643   d.1690

Thomas = Mary Osgood
1646-1712   1649/50-1705

Amesbury, MA

| Hannah 1670/71- 1699/00 | Thomas 1671- 1750 | Captin Richard = 1673-1747 Dorothy Barnard (11 Children) | Samuel 1674/5- 1735 | Mary 1676- 1766 | Anne b.1678- 1766 | William b.c. 1680/81 | John b.c. 1682/3 | Joseph b.c. 1685/6 | Benjamin b.1688 | Ebenezer b.1690 | Daniel b.1692 |

So. Hampton, NH
1695-1737

| David = 1695/6-prior to 1748 Keziah Colby | Captain Jonathon = 1698/9-1762 Ann Challis (10 children) Judith Williams (2 Children) | Hannah 1701- 83 | John b. 1704 | Dorothy b. 1706 | Richard b. 1708/9 | Miriam b. 1711 | Moses b.c. 1713 | Aaron b. 1716 | Barnard b. 1719 | Mary b. 1722 |

So.Hampton,
NH

| Richard b. 1723 | Cpt. John 1726- | Edmund b.1733 1806 | Philip 1722/3- | Challis b.1724 1773 | Jonathon 1726- | Mary 1729/30 1819 | Mary b. 1731 | Judith b. 1733 | Dorothy b. 1735 | Anne b. 1739 | Lydia b. 1740 | Susannah b.c. 1740/1 | Thomas = b.1745 Dorothy | Miriam b.1747 |

Topsham,
Vermont

| David 1769-1839 | Jonathon b.1771 | Richard b.1773 | Thomas b.1776 | Joshua 1778-1871 | Moses = 1784-1845 Mary Carter 1787-1875 (11 Children) | Aaron b.1787 |

Almont, MI

| Thomas Jefferson 1806-69 | Bagley 1808-75 | Frederick P. 1812-1900 | Parmelia 1812-94 | Emeline B. 1814-91 | Mary Jane 1816-91 | Elizabeth 1818-96 | Moses 1822-83 | Harriet E. 1825-28 | Richard 1827-94 | James C. b.1830 |

sided home as a tangible legacy of his creativity.

The octagon house he built in Almont in the early 1850s stands as a unique centerpiece for a story that will carry into the 21st century. Physically, the octagon architectural style itself marks an interesting point in the evolution of building trends in America. Also, because the survival of the Currier octagon in Almont is assured, the house serves as a stage to dramatize the life and times of the Currier family and the town in which the structure is located.

Roots of this tri-partite story were planted in 1616 in Salisbury, England, where Richard Currier, the first Currier to settle in America, was born. More than three centuries later, the line continues producing men and women whose names are recorded in social, political, industrial and literary history from New England to Michigan.

Richard's son, Thomas, followed, then a grandson, Richard, and a great-grandson, Moses. Moses' sons, Frederick Plumer Moses Jr., and Richard headed for Michigan in the 1840s. Four generations later, Frederick Plumer Currier IV continued the Currier saga by his commitment to restore the Currier Octagon in Almont.

---

4. Henry Curryer genealogy chart
This genealogy chart shows the eight generations beginning with Henry Curryer in England down to the eleven children of Moses Currier, three of whom came to Michigan, Frederick, Moses and Richard. Charts for the descendants of Frederick, Richard and Moses are shown later in the book.

Evidence points to Henry Curryer as the father of Thomas Currier, but it is not conclusive.

It took the Curriers seven generations to move from Amesbury, Massachusetts to Almont, Michigan; each generation continued to move westward as the country steadily expanded.

Richard Currier Comes to America c.1640

Richard was born March 3, 1616, and baptized in St. Thomas Parish Church, Salisbury, England, in the same year. The son of Thomas Currier of Salisbury, England, Richard came to America around 1640 and was one of the founders of Amesbury, Massachusetts, home of John Greenleaf Whittier. The records show that Richard Currier made the first of many land purchases there in 1641 and 1642.

Richard Currier, his Life and Times

The records, however, do not show that Richard assumed the occupation suggested by his name. A "currier" is one who stretches leather, receiving it from the tanner and transferring it to the cordwainer or shoemaker for final production. A cordwainer worked with cordovan, a soft, fine-grained, dark grayish-brown leather from the inner layer of a horse's rump.[1] Although Richard did not pursue the trade of "currier," it is probable that a remote ancestor was so engaged when last names were assigned centuries before in England.

Richard Currier assumed a position of prominence in the Amesbury community. His name frequently appears in the deed records as having made land purchases; his occupations are listed as planter and millwright. He became actively involved in community affairs and was town clerk in 1654–55.[2] In the seating of the Amesbury Church (or meeting house as it then was called) his name appears first to "set at the table." The most prominent citizens of the community occupied the front seats in the church.

New Englanders faced tremendous political and social upheaval as they struggled for settlement and land purchases with the Native Americans. The Rhode Island Narragansett Indians war against the British colonists, for instance, was brought on by the assassination of a prominent Narragansett tribal leader. This was King Philip's War (1675–1691). The Indians nearly wiped out settlements at Plymouth and Massachusetts Bay. When fighting escalated, local militiamen were brought in from the Connecticut Colony, and the New England Confederation declared war. Richard Currier participated in the war effort despite his age. He became a soldier at 60!

His wartime role proved to be an asset for his descendants, who drew land in Narragansett Township No. 1 in York County, Maine, based on rights conveyed to him for his military service.

After Ann's death in 1676, Richard Currier married Johana Pinder who had been twice widowed, on October 26, 1676. They had two children, Hannah and Thomas. At some point Richard Currier moved to Salisbury, Massachusetts, a neighboring community of Amesbury located to the southeast near the Atlantic coast. He died there on February 22, 1686.

The Currier line continues through Thomas, born in Amesbury, March 3, 1646. Like his father, Thomas owned land in Amesbury, and he continued the family tradition of community service by acting as town clerk in 1674 and later. He also served as deacon of the local church. On December 9, 1668 he married Mary Osgood whose father owned a sawmill in Salisbury.

When Mary's father deeded her half of his sawmill in 1697, Thomas became the owner and operator. Thomas and Mary had 12 children, nine sons and three daughters.[3] Deacon Thomas Currier died in Amesbury on September 17, 1712.

---

5. FPC I genealogy chart

The descendants of FPC I from his marriage with Mary P. Clark, total eighteen people at the fifth generation level. Interestingly none of these descendants now carry the last name Currier. In total, his descendants, living and dead, equal forty two.

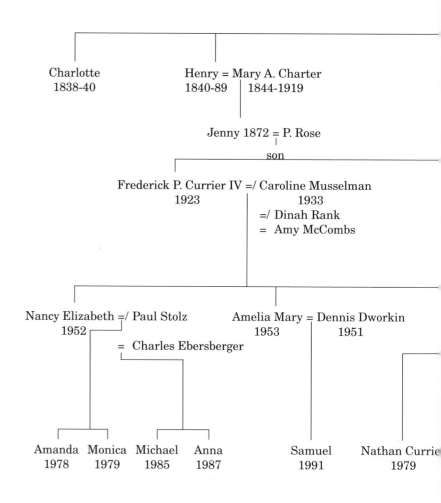

Charlotte
1838-40

Henry = Mary A. Charter
1840-89 | 1844-1919

Jenny 1872 = P. Rose

son

Frederick P. Currier IV =/ Caroline Musselman
1923 | 1933
=/ Dinah Rank
= Amy McCombs

Nancy Elizabeth =/ Paul Stolz
1952
= Charles Ebersberger

Amelia Mary = Dennis Dworkin
1953 | 1951

Amanda 1978 Monica 1979 Michael 1985 Anna 1987

Samuel 1991

Nathan Currie 1979

= Married
=/ Divorced

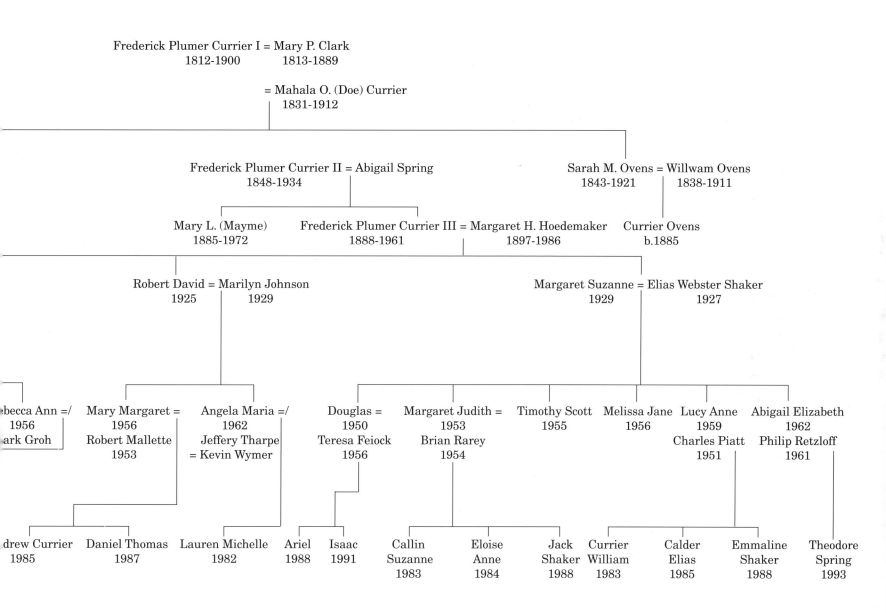

Frederick Plumer Currier I = Mary P. Clark
1812-1900   1813-1889

= Mahala O. (Doe) Currier
1831-1912

Frederick Plumer Currier II = Abigail Spring   Sarah M. Ovens = Willwam Ovens
1848-1934   1843-1921   1838-1911

Mary L. (Mayme)   Frederick Plumer Currier III = Margaret H. Hoedemaker   Currier Ovens
1885-1972   1888-1961   1897-1986   b.1885

Robert David = Marilyn Johnson   Margaret Suzanne = Elias Webster Shaker
1925   1929   1929   1927

becca Ann =/   Mary Margaret =   Angela Maria =/   Douglas =   Margaret Judith =   Timothy Scott   Melissa Jane   Lucy Anne   Abigail Elizabeth
1956   1956   1962   1950   1953   1955   1956   1959   1962
ark Groh   Robert Mallette   Jeffery Tharpe   Teresa Feiock Brian Rarey   Charles Piatt Philip Retzloff
                 1953   = Kevin Wymer   1956   1954   1951   1961

drew Currier   Daniel Thomas   Lauren Michelle   Ariel   Isaac   Callin   Eloise   Jack   Currier   Calder   Emmaline   Theodore
1985   1987   1982   1988   1991   Suzanne   Anne   Shaker   William   Elias   Shaker   Spring
                                                                          1983   1984   1988   1983   1985   1988   1993

The Currier family continued to live and flourish in Amesbury. Thomas and Mary's son, Richard, was born there on April 12, 1673. Appropriately called "Captain," he owned and ran a shipyard in Amesbury on the Merrimack River, although his occupation was recorded as "yeoman," or "independent farmer".[4] On August 29, 1695, Richard married Dorothy Barnard (1674–1765), also of Amesbury. They had 11 children, all of whom married.

Little information has been located regarding Captain Richard Currier, yet he must have led a busy and lucrative life because there were continuous shipments into the Massachusetts interior from his yard. He died in Amesbury on February 8, 1747 or 1748.

Captain John Currier Breakfasts with General George Washington

Richard's three grandsons (by a son, David) fought in the American Revolutionary War. One of them, Captain John Currier (1726–1803) led a company of militiamen in Colonel Isaac Merrill's regiment that fought at Bunker Hill. For his valiant leadership, Captain John Currier was asked to have breakfast with General George Washington at Cambridge, Massachusetts, on October 26, 1775.

Another of Richard's sons, Jonathan, also was a captain. Born on February 7, 1698, in Amesbury, he married Ann Challis (also of Amesbury) in February 1721, or 1722. They had 11 children. A son Theophilus served with Isaac Sherman's army in the American Revolutionary War. After Ann's death on July 25, 1742, Jonathan married Judith Williams on April 19, 1744 They had two children, a daughter Miriam and a son Thomas, through whom the line to the first Frederick Plumer continues. Captain Jonathan Currier died October 30, 1762, in South Hampton, New Hampshire, and is buried in the Currierville Cemetery there.

Jonathan's son, Thomas, was born on March 14, 1745, in South Hampton. There is no record of Thomas' occupation, although he is referred to as "Deacon" which suggests he was actively involved in the church. Thomas married Dorothy Bagley, and they had eight children, among them a son, Moses. Deacon Thomas Currier died in South Hampton on March 23, 1812, and is also buried in the Currierville Cemetery.

Moses Currier brings the lineage directly to the Curriers of Almont. Born June 1, 1784 in South Hampton, Moses married Mary Carter (August 13, 1784–May 24, 1875) of Kingston, New Hampshire, on August 13, 1805. They had 11 children. Harriet E. died at the age of three. Her early death was rare among the Curriers who were generally a healthy family. Few Currier children died at childbirth or within the first few years, as was often the sad case.

Settlement in New England was well established by the mid-18th century, opening the way for visionaries to explore the country's unknown interior. Among them were Moses' sons, Frederick Plumer, Moses Jr., and Richard, who headed for Michigan in search of new opportunities. Their father never had the opportunity to travel with them. He died June 22, 1845, and was buried in the Currier Hill Cemetery, Topsham, Vermont.

The legacy of the Curriers in New England is impressive and is immortalized on their tombstones dotting its landscape. Frederick Plumer Currier and his family would broaden that legacy with their achievements in Michigan.

Frederick P. Currier I, his Early Years

Frederick P. Currier was born in Newbury Township,

Orange County, Vermont, in 1812. His twin sister Permelia H.—who died on her 82nd birthday in 1894—never married.

Frederick lived on the family farm until he was 19 when he began working odd jobs by the month until he attended Newbury Seminary and Adkinson Seminary in New Hampshire. After his seminary experience, he learned the carpenter and joiner trade. In his early twenties he worked as a shoemaker in Haverhill, Massachusetts. He hired a number of skilled workmen and ran a shop of his own during the winter months, devoting his summers to masonry work.

He followed his successful venture as a shoemaker by returning to Newbury to establish a partnership in brick manufacturing with a man named Keys, thus adding to the variety of occupations that prepared him well for his entrepreneurial pursuits in Michigan.

On November 7, 1837, Frederick married Mary P. Carter (1813–1889) of New Hampshire. They had four children: Charlotte died before age one; Henry was born April 23, 1840; Frederick P. Currier Jr. on September 26, 1848, and Sarah, December 26, 1843.

These Curriers lived in Topsham where Frederick built and operated a large tannery with his brother Moses. Born in Topsham on June 1, 1822, Moses Jr. married Mahala Doe (1831–1912) on March 28, 1850. They had four children.[5]

Selling his interest to Moses, Frederick farmed for a year before, at age 32, he became captivated with tales of Michigan's wilderness and set out with his brother on an exploratory trip. Interestingly, Frederick's migration and venturesome decision to make Michigan his home reversed traditional roles, for he was 10 years older than brother Moses when they made their first trip to Michigan in 1842. Travel between New England and Michigan was made relatively easier by the open-ing of the Erie Canal in the 1820s. Apparently, Frederick followed that water route often after his and Moses' initial visit to Michigan. Frederick eventually decided to stay, while Moses returned to New England and resumed his career there. (Oral family history notes that Frederick moved to Michigan permanently because Mary had tuberculosis and the "pine air" of Michigan was thought to be beneficial to those who suffered from the disease).

Frederick and Moses had established some business enterprises in Lapeer County, particularly in response to the lumbering needs of its new settlements. Between 1842 and 1845 Frederick had built a large steam sawmill in Imlay for the Beach, Imlay & Morse Company and operated a paper mill in Vermont.

Currier probably built several mills for which he is not credited. His extensive land holdings—particularly after 1849, when he had established himself in Almont—were located adjacent to creeks, the main power source for mills.[6]

The Great Starch Factory

In 1846 Currier worked as a millwright and built a factory to manufacture starch, an enterprise that kept local farmers busy harvesting potatoes. The project proved so successful that Mary and children moved to Michigan in 1847. Letters of Horatio W. Shaw to his brother and sister in the 1845–1848 period included a reference to Currier's starch factory: "What would the farmers say to a proposition to furnish the 100,000 bushels of potatoes a year for 10 years at 10 cents a bushel and draw them to town?" he wrote. "A merchant of Almont once entered into written contract to do that very thing and the farmers took up the task. This was to supply the Great Starch Factory which was built down near the brook." [7]

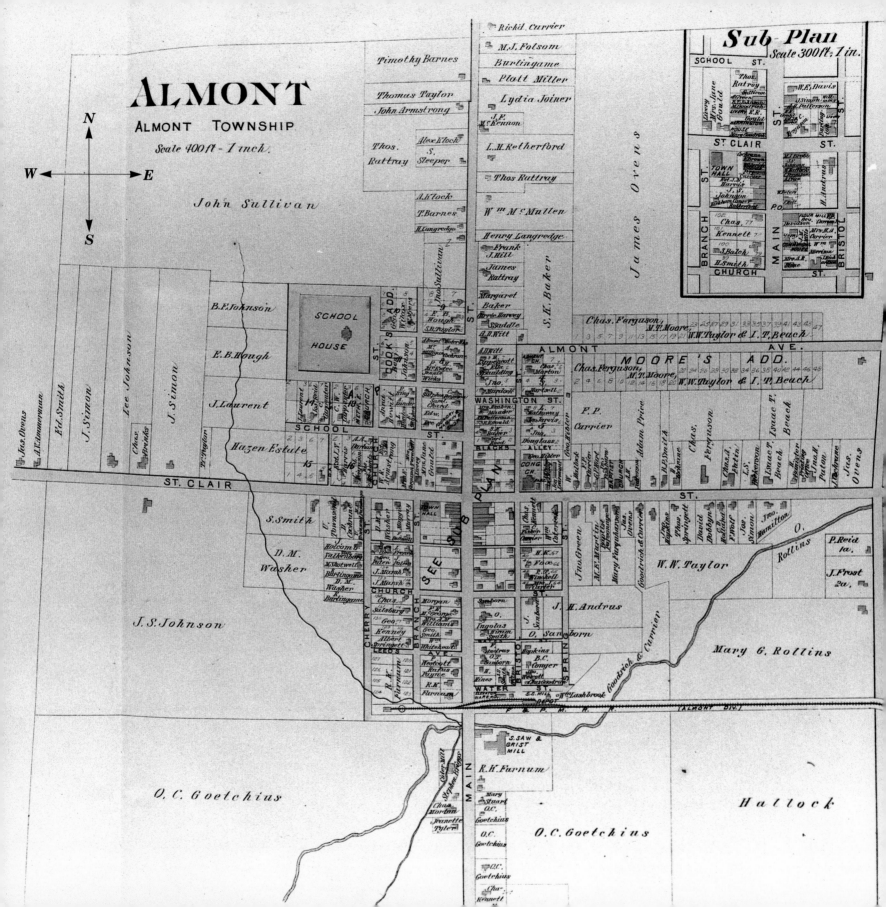

ALMONT

ALMONT TOWNSHIP

Scale 400 ft = 1 inch.

Records of the 1850 Almont census show that $1,000 was invested in the starch factory; it employed 26 males. Sixteen tons of starch were produced in that year from 5,000 bushels of potatoes. However, the business ran its course and was sold in 1851 to Briggs and Teller who turned the building into a flour mill and upright saw and planing mill. The structure still stands at Kings Cider Mill on South Main Street in Almont.

Through his starch factory project, Currier established himself as a creative and visionary entrepreneur. He also became involved with another project—a foundry that had been established in 1844 by J.P. Muzzy and Barrows. In 1851 Currier bought out Barrows, and Muzzy and Currier established a consolidated foundry and machine business.

Joel Muzzy is listed in the 1850 Federal census as having invested $1,500 in the company. In that year, 10 tons of iron valued at $200 were utilized as raw materials. He and Frederick manufactured 200 "ploughs" valued at $1,500 and 50 stoves valued at $500. Muzzy and Currier used real horsepower and also employed 26 men. The business moved to a building constructed on the site formerly occupied by Price and Hendershot on North Main Street.

Lapeer's First Steam Engine

Currier furnished the greatest part of the capital for the firm's manufacture of furnaces and other machines. The first steam engine built in Lapeer

---

6. Early Almont Township Map from Beer's Atlas, 1893
This map shows the location of Frederick P. Currier I's Octagon home and acreage. During construction of the Currier Octagon, the family lived in a house just east of the building site. Frederick P. Currier I's oldest son Henry's home is located near the agricultural implement factory. Richard's home (the younger son) is located on the far north end of Main Street.

County was produced using horse-power in Muzzy and Currier's shop in 1853. William Rider was the head machinist. The foundry and machine business continued well into the second half of the century. In fact, Currier installed furnaces from his own foundry in his newly-built octagon home.

The Curriers of England, Massachusetts, Vermont and Michigan were hard-working individuals with the character and integrity to become leaders in their respective communities. Their active pursuit of a wide array of business interests made invaluable contributions to the growth of every area in which they resided.

Indeed, Frederick P. Currier's early efforts set the stage for Almont's expansion in the second half of the 19th century.

Footnotes

1. This leather also is obtained from pigs and goats.

2. David W. Hoyt, *The Old Families of Salisbury and Amesbury, Massachusetts* (Providence, RI, 1898) 118

3. Nathaniel Currier of the famous printing team of Currier and Ives is the descendant of their son, Thomas.

4. Hoyt, 120.

5. Moses Jr. and Mahala's son, Moses Alonzo, continue the Currier line. Their descendants are currently researching the genealogy and were of great help in contributing to this document.

6. Early land purchases in Almont Township by Currier: 1842 part of section 22 (This is the property on which the octagon house was built); 1850, part of sections 7 and 21; 1851 part of village lots 2, 8 and 29 and part of section 20; 1852 village lot number 3; 1854 part of section 20; 1858 part of village lot number 5.

7. The Shaw Papers, Michigan Historical Collections, Bentley Historical Library, The University of Michigan.

CHAPTER TWO

Almont, the Early Years

By the time the Curriers settled in Almont in the 1840s, Michigan's population had grown from a mere 8,927 in 1820 to 212,267 in 1840. The territory achieved statehood status during these two decades of rapid development. In the process, the state overcame a surveyor's devastating report that suggested its hinterlands were virtually uninhabitable.

Joseph Wampler, a surveyor from Ohio, was selected to map the land that now includes Saginaw, Tuscola, Huron, Sanilac, St. Clair, Lapeer and Genesee counties. Wampler reported to Congress that nothing grew in Michigan but small scrubby oaks and that it was habitable only by mosquitoes, bull frogs and Indians. With deep, narrow streams and swamps, Wampler declared that Michigan's land was so poor that not

7. Stump puller with man
This massive iron screw machine used horse power to slowly winch large stumps out of the ground. Many of these stump pullers were sold to farmers in the Thumb region by The Currier Agricultural Works. A small scale model of this stump puller is still among the Currier family's possessions.

more than one acre in a thousand was tillable. In light of these negative reports, it was ironic that farming would become Lapeer County's principal activity. In 1872, the county was the site of Michigan's first local grange.[1]

The fertile soils were deposited by Michigan's numerous rivers and creeks, and Ice Age glaciers sculpted the rolling countryside. Lapeer county alone has some 140 freshwater inland lakes.

Disappearance of the glaciers left the county's land surface covered with marshy swamps and forests so thick that the early settlers could travel for miles and barely see the sunlight. The county of Lapeer was established in 1831, but settlers had begun to arrive ten years earlier.[2] Travel across these lowlands was extremely arduous for the early settlers, their wagons loaded with personal possessions, newborn babies and small children.

The scope of their problems was captured by Mary Ingalls Bristol who wrote her "Recollections and Memoirs" of a trip from Detroit to Almont in 1836. "People were kind and helped each other," she reported, "for all that had loaded wagons had to be helped. There were no roads, only mud. The water in the worst place almost reached our lumber box and there was nearly three miles of that. We started on our way, Father with the sick babe in his arms, Orson driving the oxen and cows, and Emily with my poor, tired mother and me in the one-horse wagon." They eventually arrived in Almont, all but the baby who died the day after they left Detroit.[3]

Whenever possible, wagon loads of settlers traveled and worked together to cut through the thick, hardwood-conifer forests. Roads were constructed of logs placed across the muddy swamp areas. Weary and frustrated, settlers also confronted wolves, bears, wildcats and mosquitoes. Many became discouraged and turned back; the hardy forged on to settle Almont, some 50 miles north of Detroit, the state's most populous area.

The Miami Indians

In Almont they found a thriving Indian population. Bands of Chippewas and Miamis roamed the area. A large willow tree on the south side of West St. Clair Street near the brook served as the Indians' sacred meeting place on yearly visits to Almont. Ca-yu-ga-ha-go, chief of the Miamis, was buried along the banks of the Almont brook called Shus-hu-ga by the Indians.[4] This brook is the north branch of the Clinton River, much smaller today, but still the same waterway.

Early settlers lived peacefully with the Indians who would come into town with beads, moccasins, baskets, berries, furs, buckskins and venison to trade for tobacco, bright cloth and alcohol at John Robert's Trading Store (141 South. Main). Tip-si-co, a Huron, frequently visited Almont to exchange stories with the townspeople and in 1909 attended Almont's first homecoming.

Early Almont Settlers

The oldest town in Lapeer county, Almont had its first settlers in 1827 when William Allen, his son G.W. Allen, and James Worthington cut a road through the wilderness north of what is now Main Street. In 1828 Lydia Chamberlain made the first land purchase in Almont Township, but she never settled on the prop-

---

8. Stump fence
This image, captured by Lewis Fitch, demonstrates the inventive temperament of the early settlers of Almont. A common sight throughout Michigan in the 1850's and 60's were these huge hardwood stump fences which often stretched the length of large fields and required little maintenance.

erty. That same year James Deneen came from Ohio, purchasing 80 acres in Section 9.[5]

Oliver and Bezaleel Bristol arrived in 1830, and built the first frame house within the town limits. Simple home construction continued, Daniel Black building the first log structure in 1833. Recognizing the need for a meeting place to fill the community's social needs, Black obtained a license in Pontiac for $18 to establish the town's first tavern.

Records of the township's early organization were destroyed by fire on March 29, 1842, but it is known that Almont's first town meeting was held in Daniel Black's tavern.[6] Ira S. Sanders, justice of the peace, presided. Thirteen voters were present and elected Oliver Bristol as supervisor, Jonathan Sleeper, clerk, Daniel Black, treasurer, Nicholas Richardson and Elisha Webster, assessors, and James Deneen, highway commissioner.

An influx of Scottish immigrants in 1833 further boosted Almont's population. David Taylor, John Hopkins, James Thompson and William Robertson established the Scotch settlement in the southeast section of Almont Township. Several Scottish surnames remain associated with historic settlers' houses on West St. Clair Street.

The population spurt led to the community's organization on March 7, 1834, under the name Mia, which Elisha Webster suggested in honor of his daughter. Mia was soon changed to Bristol to honor the first supervisor, Oliver Bristol.

Bristol was organized as a township in 1837, the same year Michigan became a state. The village of

---

9. Currier Octagon c. 1890
Frederick P. Currier I in a favorite chair on the gracious east porch which, along with the wrought iron fence, is an important part of the octagon aesthetic.

Newburgh within that township consisted of five residential dwellings, schoolhouse, store, blacksmith shop, shoe shop and grist mill servicing the subsistence farming community. The two names became confusing and Almont was chosen and adopted in 1846 about the time Frederick P. Currier was preparing to move his family from Vermont.

How Almont was Named
Local tradition is that "Almont" was suggested by James Thompson who donated the clock that is located in the tower of the Congregational Church. The choice of name, in effect honoring Juan Almonte, a Mexican general, reflected some strong feeling against United States' participation in a Mexican War (1845–48). General Almonte had fought with General Santa Ana at the Battle of the Alamo in Texas in 1836, and 10 years later was Mexican ambassador to the United States. He resigned the post in 1845 to protest attempts by the U.S. government to annex Texas. (Those New Englanders with abolitionist tendencies feared that a "liberated" Texas would become a territory of slave expansion.)

Many Americans did not sympathize with the policy of the government and felt that war could have been avoided. Apparently James Thompson and other citizens of Bristol were supporters of this anti-war sentiment, including issues of slavery and acquisition of territorial lands.

Construction of improved roads and a stagecoach line brought more people into Almont, an area which in 1840 would boast a population of 888 (444 males and 444 females).

Availability of goods and services expanded with increased settlement. Dr. Caleb Carpenter, Almont's first doctor, set up his office in 1834. He also served as the foreman of the jury when the first circuit court was established October 17, 1837.

The year 1835 saw the first groceries sold by Lewis Alverson and the first general store established by Charles Keeler. Albert Southwell ran the first blacksmith shop. The first wagon shop was built by Beach and Rundell in 1840. Silas McKeen began to practice law in Almont in 1846, the same year that McGeorge and Cardwill opened the town's first hardware and tin shop. They were followed by another hardware entrepreneur, R.I. Goetchius. In 1850 shoemaker Thomas Chapman manufactured 500 pairs of boots and 200 pairs of shoes.

The main source of power for many of these industries was water, and several mills sprang up along the creeks that ran through Almont. Carding and fanning mills were opened in 1834. Elisha Webster also built a grist mill. A plank road from Almont to Mount Clemens led to increased settlement, resulting in the opening of a steam grist and sawmill in 1851 and planing mills in 1854. Lumbermen were attracted to Almont's pines and hardwood. As mentioned earlier, Beach, Imlay, and Morse established a large steam sawmill in Imlay in 1844, with machinery built by Frederick Currier.

Uprooted from their eastern foundations, the new Westerners found it necessary to incorporate their value system into social institutions compatible with their environment. Along with their oxen, Almont's early settlers brought a strong belief in a higher power and the religious tenets which they practiced in their New England and European towns. It was common for itinerant preachers to be sent out to the wilderness by mother churches to organize and establish congregations. One came to Almont.

The Reverend Luther Shaw was Almont's first preacher, sent as a missionary in 1830 by the eastern (U.S.) churches. He conducted services in a small schoolhouse and also established a settlement on the northern boundary of Almont Township known as Belle Arbor (located near where the Mark Farely farm stands today on Ross Road). That settlement soon began to disband as people developed fevers due to vapors from decaying organic matter or a "miasma" created by the lethargic Belle River. Many died and were buried in Webster Cemetery. Healthy ones moved to Almont, Reverend Shaw among them. The settlement was almost completely abandoned by 1836. The small church at Belle Arbor later became affiliated with Almont's Congregational Church.

Early Religious Organizations

Almont's first religious service, however, had been conducted by Reverend Abel Warren in 1829, a year before Shaw's arrival. Associated with the Methodist Episcopal Church, Warren held funeral services for the infant son of Oliver and Bezaleel Bristol. He preached in Lapeer and other surrounding counties and performed the first wedding ceremony on January 15, 1832, joining Cullen Baldwin and Nancy Elderkin.

The Methodist Episcopal Society was organized in the 1840s. Services were held in a small frame building on the northwest corner of West St. Clair and Church streets. The building later was used as a school, then moved a short distance to the north where it was remodeled into a residence which still stands at 115 Church Street. A one-and one-half story Greek Revival structure built around 1867 served as the Methodist Episcopal Church parsonage. It remains today at 303 West St. Clair and is included in the West St. Clair Historic District.

As the Methodist church continued to expand, a large brick edifice was built in the second half of the 19th century. The pews from the old church were sold to a church in Pontiac and the bell moved to Woodmere

Methodist Episcopal Church in Detroit where it still rings.

The New Congregational Church

For the Curriers, attention was focused on the Almont Congregational Church, organized on December 6, 1838. Reverend Hiram Smith conducted the first services in a log school one mile west of Almont. A wood frame structure built in 1847 on North Main and Washington Streets housed the congregation of 110 under the pastorate of Reverend Charles Kellogg. The church supported a strong congregation under several pastors until the building burned on Thanksgiving Day 1871 due to an overheated stove. Services were held temporarily in the Baptist Church.

When funding for a new Congregational Church was not adequate, Frederick Currier and James Thompson became the church's benefactors, donating $6,700. An elegant brick Gothic Church was completed in 1874. The exquisite polychrome brick structure still stands on East St. Clair Street, only a few hundred feet from the octagon house Currier had built twenty years earlier.

The Curriers' influence on the church reflected their New England roots. Congregationalism originated in Holland and became dominant in New England. Congregationalists were fiercely independent and dogmatic in their thinking. In America, they split with the Unitarians whom they considered more liberal, and they came to represent the Puritan lifestyle of the New Englanders. The Curriers were devoted members, attending church two hours every Sunday.

The other benefactor of the Congregational Church was James Thompson, a native of Scotland, who had become a resident of the Scotch settlement in 1833. It was he who suggested changing the town's name from Bristol to Almont. Thompson raised draft horses and

cattle and was a poet and humanitarian, leaving the bulk of his estate ($11,200) to Detroit's Harper Hospital. He also donated money for the clock installed along with the bell in the tower of the Congregational Church steeple on July 29, 1878. The clock has received careful attention throughout the years. In 1964 the Almont Garden Club raised $2,000 to electrify and rebuild it. At the same time, the bell's striker was repositioned to increase the intonation of sound.

The United Presbyterian Church was organized in the town of Bruce on December 22, 1846. Some of the original members were residents of Almont, but the majority were from the Scotch settlement in south-eastern Almont Township. Services were held in a building erected by Dr. Neil Gray on his farm in Bruce. It was used as a granary after a second edifice was built in 1852, three miles north of what was the Morton Farm. The strong Scotch church tradition held the Scottish congregation and pastors together until the 1940s.

The Baptist Society was organized in 1837 under the Reverend Cyrus Churchill. Edward Hough opened his home northwest of Almont for worship services. A frame church building was erected on East St. Clair Street in 1847 on a lot purchased by Solon T. Spafford. In 1898 the church was remodeled and an addition constructed on the west end. The frame Greek Revival church still stands with its graceful Palladian stained glass windows located in the center of the building.

Five Cemeteries

Almont's history is further reflected in the names on tombstones in various early cemeteries. Five are located on Almont's outskirts on plots of land originally purchased by the town or individual families.

The Currier family and others assisted a committee

that bought four acres of the southeast corner of Ebenezer Hough's farm in 1854. Named the Almont Cemetery, it is located on Hough Road across from property still owned by the Hough family. The first plots, auctioned off at $6 a lot and $3 for half a lot, were purchased by Samuel Price, E.B. Shaw, James Ovens, James Taylor, Bancroft Taylor, W.K. Hough, Witherale and Ebenezer Hough, John Wells, Daniel Black, B.F. Johnston, and William Rider. F.P. Currier and other Currier family members are buried there.

The Sand Hill Cemetery, located west of town on Sand Hill Road, was established in 1841 by the Union Interring Society and lots were sold for a few shillings. The society purchased spades, shovels, straps, hoes, bar and pall cloth, necessary items for proper internment. The earliest burial was that of Abigail King, on August 25, 1834. Other burials before 1850 were of Joshua Sutton, Hannah Wilber, Edward Bancroft, Captain Parmeler Allen, A. Blanchard, Daniel Freeman and wife, Caleb Gilert and Harriet J.S. Vannatter.

Land for the Ferguson Cemetery located on the northeast corner of Tubspring and Kidder Roads—then part of the Ferguson farm—was purchased on May 20, 1848. A memorial to the late Charles D. Ferguson was erected in this cemetery. Earliest burials were of Albert Southwell 1839, Henry Sleeper 1842, infant son Sleeper 1849 and Ernest Wells 1851.

Some early settlers buried in the Webster Cemetery (named for W.S. Webster) are Cardwell, Churchill, Greenman, Hayward, Harvey, Hannah, Hough, Howland, Freeman, Owen, Parmelee, Pearsell, Rogers, Shaw, Walker and Wilcox. The cemetery is four miles north of town on Webster Road.

Goodrich Cemetery, located on Kidder Road, in Bruce Township, still has its original iron fence. Among the recognizable names of early settlers found there are Bishop, Bostick, Braidwood, Bristol, Cochrane, Fatin, Goetches, Gould, Hamilton, Ingalls, McEntee, Robertson and Shaw.

Early Educational Efforts

On a more temporal level, the Almont settlers also had a high regard for education. They moved quickly to provide funds for the construction of school houses and hiring of teachers. None of the original school houses have survived, but the effort provided a solid foundation for education in Almont.

The first schoolhouse was a log structure built on the south side of West St. Clair Street in 1834. The first school teacher, Charlotte Freeman, received boarding and a weekly salary of 75 cents. In 1836 and 1837 Elijah Bostick taught in a small frame building three miles outside of Almont. Other rural schools were set up on private property throughout Almont Township and were named for the men who owned the property.

An attempt to provide higher education was made by Reverend Eliphet Parker. He established an academy in 1844 and constructed a building sometime afterward; it still stands on East St. Clair Street, east of the old Baptist Church. The building became the property of the school district and served as the high school until 1867. The building is now privately owned.

Almont's residents, anxious to communicate with friends and relatives outside of town, paid handsomely for postal service. Dr. Caleb Carpenter rode his horse

10. Early street map of Almont from the F.A. Dunham Atlas 1893
This map shows the proximity of the Congregational Church in relation to Frederick P. Currier's Octagon house, which is next to the homes of his two sons.

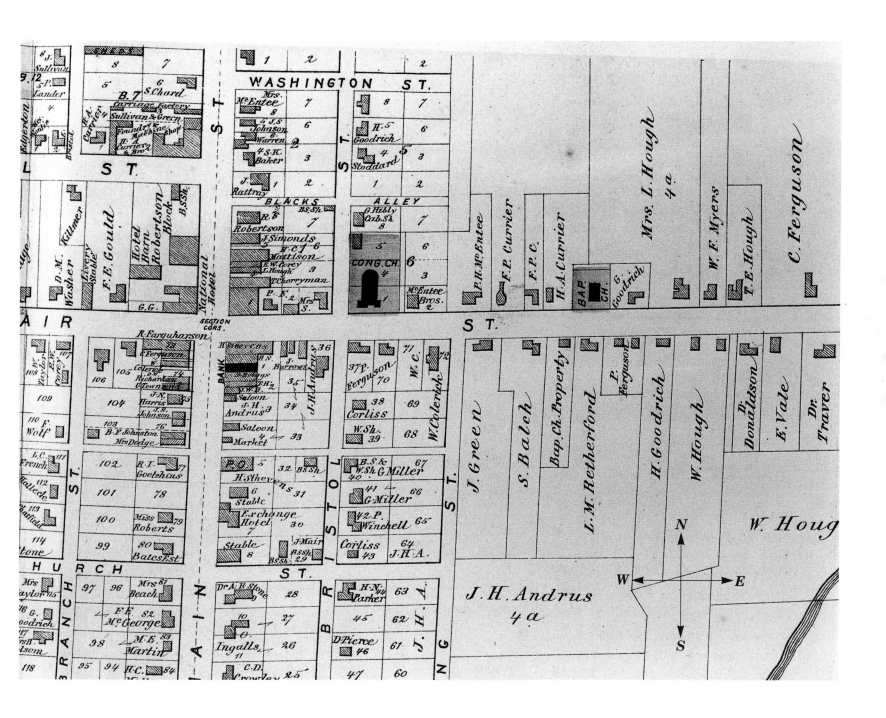

to Royal Oak once a week to pick up the mail, often through hazardous weather conditions and over bad roads. People paid 20 cents for each letter received, although postage in larger towns with good road access was one cent and soon after raised to two cents.

The first post office was established in Dr. Carpenter's house in 1835. Ezra Hazen became postmaster in 1838. The building on the corner of South Main and Mill Streets was the post office at one time. Built in the 1880s, it is the oldest frame building to have survived Almont's fires. A proposal to move it to Flint in the early 1980s was led by the Almont Historical Society and Kay Hurd, but was unsuccessful. Recognizing possible threats to their community's heritage, the group reorganized and has since conducted house tours and lectures on Almont's history. The group is particularly proud of the 1983 listing of West St. Clair Street as a National Register Historic District.

What is now Almont emerged from a forest-covered wilderness into a bustling community that by 1850 had gradually changed from dependency on subsistence farming and milling into a lumbering and manufacturing center.

The Curriers' octagon house, along with the many current Almont-area historic farms, are links to the past. Farms in the Almont area that have been occupied by the same family for at least 100 years or more, and are therefore eligible for official "Centennial Farm" designation by the Michigan Historical Commission, are the following:

Centennial Farms
The Bishop Home—6930 Boardman Road, Almont. Truman Bishop purchased this 185-acre farm on November 21, 1836, for $500. The frame upright and wing house was built in 1855. It has remained in the Bishop family. Leon and Emma Bishop occupied the house in 1954. Emma passed away in January 1977.

The Braidwood Home—8290 Boardman Road, Bruce Township. This farm, located on the border of Lapeer and Macomb counties, was purchased by Alexander Braidwood, a Scottish immigrant, in 1843. The farm and elegant upright and wing house was occupied by Norman Braidwood and his family until they moved into town in the 1980s. It was designated a Centennial Farm on April 25, 1967.

The Farley Home—3120 Farley Road, Almont. Mark Farley purchased this property in 1859. Once called "Whey Island," the large dairy operation was run by Charles K. Farley and his sons, Fred, Mark and Ronald. James and Mary Farley purchased the property from Ronald Farley in 1954.

The Hamilton Home—5807 Scotch Settlement Road, Almont. John Hamilton from Scotland purchased this farm in 1841. The farm sold in 1931 to Albert Desmit.

The Hough Homes—7224 and 7170 Hough Road, Almont. The wide plank board house on the Hough farm was built in 1863 by Walter Hough. The house was moved east across the orchard in 1865 when a larger house was built at 7170 Hough Road. Houghs still occupy both houses, Gretchen Hough at 7224 and Tom Hough at 7170.

The late 19th century Spangler home, two miles west of Almont, was built on land purchased by Christopher Spangler in 1842. It stands at the corner of Sand Hill and General Squire (West St. Clair) Roads and is still owned by the Spangler family.

These centennial homesteads reflect the wide variety of backgrounds of Almont's residents and the diversified economy and manufacturing bases of the city. The Currier octagon embodies the creativeness and determination of Frederick Plumer Currier who helped nurture this spirit of progress.

Footnotes

1. This information is included on the State Historical Marker situated in front of the Lapeer County Courthouse.

2. Lapeer County borrowed its name from the French "La Pierre," a translation of the Indian name for the Flint River.

3. Hildamae Waltz Bowman, *Almont, The Tale of Then and Now* (Almont, Mich., 1985) 24.

4. Ibid., 6.

5. Nellie Veness, "Almont, Michigan," *Flint Genealogical Quarterly,* Vol. 9, No. 4 (1967), 88–89.

6. H.R. Page, *History of Lapeer County, Michigan* (Chicago, Ill, 1884) 13.

CHAPTER 3

Octagons: Making a Home in Michigan

Considering the Currier Octagon specifically and other octagons across the state, questions about this unique type of house are inevitable. What makes the octagon unique? Where did the idea come from? When was it popular? Why did the popularity fade, and why do we not see more octagons across the American landscape?

The octagon shape, as it applies to the architectural form, is characterized by eight consecutively-angled exterior walls. But the walls do not necessarily have to be of the same length. Buildings with fewer, or more, than eight walls, or that have angled walls broken by straight walls, are polygonal or "many-sided."

The octagon form as an architectural design did not originate in the 19th century, nor was it spawned in America, as commonly believed. The earliest octagon, built by the Greeks in 300 B.C., was called the Tower

---

11. The Andrus Octagon
The Andrus Octagon, located in Washington Township on old Van Dyke Road in Macomb County, is a rare brick octagon based very closely on the Fowler concept. In the last few years it has been extensively restored with local and state support.

of the Winds. The technique was later applied to an octagonal church built in Pisa in 1120 A.D. The octagon form became popular in the late 16th century with the Dutch who constructed a church in Willemstad, Holland, in 1595. It still stands.

Other noteworthy examples are the 18th century powder magazine at Williamsburg, Virginia, and Poplar Forest, Thomas Jefferson's summer home, designed by him in 1819. Dutch settlers built many churches and schools in the octagon form in New Amsterdam (now New York City) in the 18th century.[1] A number of octagonal churches were built in the Hudson River valley from 1680–1750. Octagonal wings added to Adamesque-style houses were popular from 1780–1820.

The Origin of the Fowler Octagon

The octagon form—as applied to domestic residences—was popularized in America in the mid-19th century by Orson Squire Fowler, who wanted to "bring comfortable dwellings within the reach of the poorer classes." He was past the age of 40 before he presented his ideas in a book—and built an octagon of his own.

Fowler had gained national attention as a leading practitioner of phrenology (determining human character traits by examining cranial bumps). He was a well-known lecturer who absorbed ideas for the home he wanted to build for himself during "all his professional peregrinations."

Fowler was born in Cohocton, New York, October 11, 1809, and graduated from the Ashland Academy in Massachusetts in 1834. Aside from his commitment to phrenology, his eccentricity was further demonstrated by the variety of his other interests, including such subjects as family life, vegetarianism, health, sex, gardening, farming, diets, water cure, teetotalism and the octagon. He authored *Love and Parentage Applied to the Improvement of Offspring, Including Important Decisions and Suggestions to Lovers and the Married Concerning the Strongest Times and the Most Momentous Relations of Life*. It had gone through 40 printings by 1844. The equally popular sequel, *Evils and Remedies of Excessive and Perverted Sexuality, Including Warnings and Advice to the Married and Single*, also went through 40 printings.

No one is certain where and why Fowler developed his intense interest in the octagon. He owned a publishing company in Auburn, New York, and was editor of a phrenology magazine, which enabled him to disseminate his ideas to a broad sector of the population.[2]

Through his publishing Fowler illustrated that he was an uninhibited man who was willing to experiment with various ideas and was not afraid to present them to the public.

The time was right. The restless search for new architectural forms was a hallmark of the Romantic Era of the mid-19th century. Italianate, Greek, Gothic and exotic Revivals using Egyptian, Oriental and Swiss motifs are examples of styles adopted at that time. The eclecticism of architectural styles eased the acceptance of the octagon among house builders and buyers.

Fowler's primary contribution was that he "rethought the house plan in order to coordinate it through a better use of new materials and mechanics."[3] Despite his eccentricity, Fowler was very mathematical and analytical in his approach to the use of space created by the octagon form. Fowler thus, in his own way, preceded the architect Louis Sullivan in advocating that "form follows function." Fowler also suggested placing Pythagoras' maxim above the octagon entrances: "Let none but geometricians enter here."

Fowler also claimed that the spherical form enclosed more space for its surface than any other form and exceeded the square by 194 square feet, a gain of one-fifth the space. His mathematical reasoning continued: "Now since a given length of octagon wall will enclose one-fifth more space than the same length of wall in a square shape, of course you can have the same sized wall of one-fifth less money, or the wall of a home one-fifth larger for the same sum, for this gain is just as great in the foundation, siding, plastering, painting, whitewashing, etc., as in the wall proper."

Fowler's Basic Book in 1848

Fowler's flirtation with this new idea led to the publication in 1848 of *A Home For All*, or a *New, Cheap, Convenient and Superior Mode of Building*. Fowler's claim of superiority for the octagon was based on the premise that "nature's forms are mostly spherical. The octagon, by approximating the circle, encloses more space for its wall than the square, besides being more compact and available."[4]

Receiving national attention, the book was widely read by builders and homeowners. Relentless lecture tours by Fowler between 1848 and the early 1850s, designed to promote his book, contributed to its immense success. Frederick Currier may have attended one of Fowler's Michigan appearances.

After the first printing of *Home For All*, Fowler advanced the idea of using a "gravel wall," a relatively new construction material. He was first exposed to this building material in Milton, Wisconsin, in 1850, where he met Joseph Goodrich, an amateur builder who constructed a polygonal structure with concrete walls in 1844. Goodrich concocted his own mixture of lime, sand and coarse gravel which he called grout, or "gravel wall."

Fowler labeled gravel "nature's building material" because it resisted fire, saved on lumber and pre-vented vermin from entering the house. This material fit into Fowler's concept of nature and man in harmony. He said, "nature has provided a cheap and comfortable building material. It keeps out cold, heat and dampness, and grows harder with age." Fowler promoted the material as abundant, cheap and durable, enabling poor men to construct their own houses. That idea obviously caught on. In 1853 Fowler revised his *Home For All* to add his ideas of the gravel wall construction method. (Essentially Fowler's idea was an early type of concrete.) *Home For All* went through seven printings between 1848 and 1857.

Ironically, relatively few octagons were constructed of this material, but the ones that were have held up well. The majority, like Currier's, were built of wood frame. Fowler felt wood was objectionable because it burned, decayed and needed constant repair, maintenance and paint. Fowler also recognized the rapid destruction of timber resources across the country. He speculated that the rising population would cause the price of lumber to increase (which it did) and he felt brick and stone also were inappropriate because they were time-consuming to construct, were affected by frost and cold in the winter and were expensive. He pointed out that the cost of hiring a bricklayer would be $1.50–$2.50 per day, compared to $10–$15 per month to hire a laborer to construct a gravel wall home. Fowler said "to cheapen and improve human houses, and especially to bring comfortable dwellings within the reach of the poorer classes, is the object of this volume."

Gravel wall construction did reduce the cost of building, but it, too, was time consuming. All materials had to be mixed on the building site. Walls were constructed by tiers, the material being poured in between a framing of two boards. It took 24 hours to dry, after which the boards were raised to set the next tier. The notable expenditure of time required in gravel-wall construction led to a great deal of amateur experimentation because it was not widely accepted by professional builders. Before attempting such an arduous task, most home-builders turned to the more familiar wood frame and masonry construction techniques of brick and stone.

Fowler vs. Downing

In the professional world, Fowler had a notable adversary. Andrew Jackson Downing was a proponent of the Gothic Revival style and published design books in the 1840s, which presented plans for farm houses and suburban middle-class Gothic Revival cottages. Architects had traditionally designed homes for the wealthy, but Downing and Fowler were challenging that tradition; Fowler in particular, targeted his houses for the middle and lower classes, as was noted. Downing and Fowler disagreed on the use of building materials and shape, as well as decorative detailing and utilitarian versus decorative functions of all house types. Their rivalry was further dramatized by their proximity: they lived across the river from each other, Fowler having built his octagon on the east bank of the Hudson River and Downing, one of his cottages on the west bank.

Downing countered Fowler's argument in support of the economy possible in an octagon building by stating that "the more irregular the outline of a building, the more the cost is increased, because it has more exterior surface and therefore requires more wall or weather boarding, more roof, more gutters, more fixtures and more ornament." He did, however, offer a grudging tribute to the octagon: "On the other hand," he said, "irregular form has great advantages, not only in the greater beauty of effect..., but in its greater variety of sizes, forms and accommodations of apartments within."

Fowler, the pragmatist, felt that Downing placed mistaken emphasis on beauty and convenience at the expense of economy. Downing defended himself by saying: "Those who desire to combine as much economy as possible with good taste in building a residence will select a cube or rectangle for the outline of its ground plan, while those to whom expense is of less importance than convenience and picturesque effect will adopt the irregular form." Fowler made no concessions to fashionable revival styles. He felt decorative elements were superfluous to the building and an additional expense. That the octagon was more a shape than a style was reflected in the fact that various decorative elements, derived from many styles, were applied to octagon exteriors, such as Stick, Italianate and Victorian barge boards.

Although they were both proponents of building houses for the common man, Fowler and Downing never were able to resolve their differences and remained competitors. Yet, aesthetics were important to Fowler. His own home in Fishkill, New York, sat on a high knoll overlooking the Hudson River. He said in his book: "Give me a beautiful landscape and an elevated site. This also guarantees a fresh, dry atmosphere, in place of valley fogs and miasmas, together with whatever summer breeze may be afloat." Eight surfaces, he continued, admitted more sunlight into the house. "Given even-sized windows will light a room more than those a fifth larger in the octagon than in a square, first because the latter has deep, dark corners,

12. The Burt Octagon
One of the earliest octagons in Michigan was built by William Austin Burt, Michigan's first surveyor who also invented the equatorial sextant in 1856 and helped discover iron ore near Marquette, Michigan. He pushed the state legislature to construct shipping locks at Sault Ste. Marie. Burt Lake, located in the Lower Peninsula southwest of Cheboygan, was named after him.

which is not the case with the octagon and also because the octagon form makes the same gain in the depth of the rooms that it does in the length of the walls, that is, the room is more compact."[5]

Improved Light and Ventilation

The advantages of light and ventilation were in keeping with Fowler's philosophy on health. He advocated using glass whenever possible, referring to it as "nature's roofing and flooring material". Fowler's own home had a 20-foot square glass-roofed cupola crowning the stairwell. Such a room, he said, would be cool in summer, warm in winter.

Progressive in his outlook, Fowler promoted and implemented new inventions. Modifications in heating systems came about in the decade between 1840 and 1850. Iron ranges and stoves substituted for fireplaces. He recognized the increased effectiveness of a centralized heating unit and recommended the use of furnaces which, he said, were "by far better a plan for warming a house than separate fireplaces."

He also advocated the installation of a cistern in the basement pumping hot and cold water into the kitchen. "One of these cisterns connects with the copper boiler attached to the kitchen range and this descending cold water forces up the hot water to the stories above, so as to give hot and cold water to each story," he wrote. Fowler advocated other inventions such as indoor water closets, dumbwaiters and speaking tubes.

Despite Fowler's claim for innovation, the octagon had several disadvantages. It was seldom as space- and energy-efficient as he contended. Interior walls left triangles of impractical spaces with a floor plan less convenient than a square or rectangle. Although he acknowledged that irregular interior spaces were created, his suggested uses for them proved more effective on paper than in practical application. Also, the inconvenience of building in the gravel-wall construction method prompted builders to employ more traditional building materials on interior spaces.

Although the "octagon fad" had a fleeting reign, Fowler did make an important contribution. His emphasis on the octagon served as a vehicle to dramatize the affordability of the materials, thus bringing attractive residential housing within the reach of the common man for the first time.

More importantly, Fowler's ideas have survived through 100 years of different architectural types. Octagons continue to appear as vacation homes, residential and commercial buildings. (An article in a national computer magazine, *How to Plan Spaces for People and Computers*, discussed space criteria, work patterns, traffic flow and planning for further expansion. The plan was an octagon.)[6]

Several fine octagons remain standing in Michigan. Their location and type are listed on pages 48 and 49.

Two octagons located in Macomb County on Van Dyke Road and 28 Mile Road, respectively, are associated with two men who made significant contributions to Michigan's heritage. Both are exquisite examples of the octagon building form, but are privately owned and interior access is not permitted.

The Loren Andrus Octagon

The Loren Andrus Octagon is located at 57500 Van Dyke Avenue (M-53) in Section 33 of Washington Township. It was built in 1860 for Loren Andrus, an engineer who surveyed the Clinton and Kalamazoo Canal and the railroad between Port Huron and Flint. Andrus' brother-in-law, David G. Stewart, a local carpenter, handled the construction. In the late 1850s Andrus and several wealthy friends strove to outdo each other with impressive residences. Andrus surpassed his friends with originality but almost went bankrupt in the process. His ostentation must have stirred local jealousies, for there is a legend that one night an enemy of the family sowed over 90 acres of mustard seeds, which still bloom every summer to the annoyance of the present owners.

Sometimes called the "house of eights," the Andrus House not only has eight sides but eight rooms and eight-foot high windows on the lower story. Bricks used in the construction were made from clay on the Andrus farm and fired by Andrus himself. A Corinthian-columned porch surrounds seven of the eight sides, while the roof with its elegantly-scrolled brackets support an octagonal cupola with weather-board siding and a pyramidal roof. The interior woodwork and intricately carved exterior brackets and columns reflect the fine craftsmanship of the carpenters.

A dramatic spiral staircase is located at the center of the house and winds upward toward the cupola which originally was glassed in.[7] Although carpenters were only paid one dollar a day, Andrus offered to double that figure if the staircase could be completed within 100 days. Stewart completed the work in 99 days and received $200 for his accomplishment. Intricate carvings embellish the ceilings.

After Andrus' death in 1901, the house changed hands several times. In the 1930s it was a restaurant and inn. In 1945 the house was purchased by the Detroit Board of Education, made possible through a donation by Albert E. Schmidt, a Detroit businessman who wanted to train urban boys in farming techniques. Young men enrolled at Wayne State University and lived in the octagon. They attended classes at the university after morning chores and returned in the afternoon to study agriculture and care for the livestock.

The Schmidt Foundation Farm was entirely self-supporting. Income from the 90 head of Holstein cattle and 1,200 Leghorn hens paid for the students' room and board, tuition and books. Andrus would have been satisfied with the productive use of his farm and house, for he was keenly interested in the breeding of sheep for fine wool and was director of the Macomb County Agricultural Society. The Foundation Farm operated successfully until 1960 when the director, Floyd Johnson, retired and the university decided it was too expensive to continue.

The house changed ownership again several times. It was purchased by Bill and Phyllis Hamilton in 1974 and was used for a museum and craft shop and restaurant. They called it Apple Barrel Farms based on research which revealed that Jonathon Chapman ("Johnny Appleseed") planted 1,600 apple trees in Andrus' orchard which was the largest apple orchard in the United States at that time.[8] They also discovered that a basement room was used to hide slaves. The room was accessible through a trap door in the parlor or by three tunnels leading to the backyard. The tunnels were filled in with cement when the home was converted to a restaurant in the 1930s.

Unfortunately, the house was severely vandalized the same year the Hamilton's had purchased it in 1974. Crystal chandeliers were ripped out, furniture damaged and objects stolen. It remained vacant for several years, but in 1986 a $100,000 State of Michigan Equity grant was awarded for its restoration. The Washington Historical Society is now actively interested in its restoration. Interestingly, Andrus was one of the original members of the Macomb County Historical Society, founded in 1881.

The Burt-Holcomb Octagon
Another Macomb County octagon is the Burt-Holcomb home, located at 3603 28 Mile Road in Mount Vernon.

Current Locations of Octagon Homes in Michigan

County	Location	Type
BarryHastings:	884 S. Jefferson	Barn
Calhoun	Albion: 29 ½ Mile Rd., ¼ mile south of railroad track	House
	Albion: 416 E. Erie	House altered
	Athens: Burr Oak and Ave. A	House
	Battle Creek: 159 North Ave.	House
	Convis Twsp: 20125 12 Mile	House
	Homer: 6284 26 Mile Rd.	House
	Homer: SE corner Lyons Lake	House
	Marshall: Fairgrounds	Exhibit Bldg.
	Marshall: 17051 16 Mile Road	House
	Marshall: 218 S. Eagle	House
	Marshall: 11-20125 off 12-mile road	House cobblestone
Cass	Dowagiac: 518 Spuce	House-altered
Clinton	Fowler: French and Grange Roads	School
Gratiot	Alma: Bliss Road	House brick
Ingham	Dansville: 1397 E. Mason St.	Housegrout/block
Hillsdale	Jonesvile: U.S. 12 and Concord Road	House altered
	North Adams	House
Ionia	Cooks Corner	House
Jackson	Parma: 6997 Brown Road	House grout/mortar
	Spring Arbor: M60, 49283 Spring Arbor Road	Barn

Current Locations of Octagon Homes in Michigan

County	Location	Type
Kalamazoo	Kalamazoo: 925 S. Westnedge	House
	Kalamazoo: 628 S. Rose	House
Kent	Grand Rapids: 3180 E. Paris Road, S. E.	House
Lapeer	Almont: 231 E. St. Clair	House
Lenawee	Adrian: 523 S. Winter	House
	Hudson: 428 S. Church	House
Livingston	Hartland Twsp: Lonetree Road	Barn
Macomb	Mt. Vernon: 28 Mile Road west of Van Dyke	House
	Washington: 5763 Van Dyke Road	House
Mason	Eden Twsp: Hawley Road	House
Newaygo	Hesperia: South Ave.	House
Oakland	Lake Orion: 850 Pleasant Ridge	House
St. Clair	Yale	House
St. Joseph	Fawn River	House
Sanilac	Amadore: Wildcat Rd.	House
	Sandusky: 132 S. Elk	House
Shiawassee	723 Bennington Road	School
Tuscola	Mayville: 5927 Treasurer Rd.	House
Van Buren	Covert: 32 Avenue	House and barn
Washtenaw	Ypsilanti: 114 N. River Street	House
	Ypsilanti: 103 S. Huron Street	House altered
Wayne	S.E. of Plymouth 7352 Newburgh Road	House

The construction date has not been documented, but it is one of Michigan's earlier octagons. The house was built by William Austin Burt, a state surveyor renowned for inventing the solar compass. Burt moved from New York state to Macomb County in 1824 where he took up mill building and was responsible for building the Dexter Mill.[9]

In 1829 Burt took out a patent on the first typewriter. (His "typographer" did not use the individual type bar that was employed in later typewriters.) Burt failed to interest anyone in his patent and gave up his invention in 1830. However, a replica of the typographer was built by his grandson for the 1893 Colombian Exposition and can be seen today on exhibit at the Smithsonian Institution.

Burt was appointed Deputy Land Surveyor by the Federal government in 1833. In 1834 he began surveying Michigan's Upper Peninsula and an area north of Milwaukee in the Wisconsin Territory. The surveys at this time were done with a magnetic compass, which was disrupted by local mineral deposits. Renewing his interest in inventions, Burt began work on a model of his solar compass in 1835, then called a "variation apparatus" or "variation compass." Variation referred to the amount of difference between true north and magnetic north. On February 26, 1836, he received patent number 9428X for his invention. The principle behind the solar compass was based on the sun dial. The surveyor used the sun as a fixed point. The sun reflected on the instrument's silver plates. An arm on the compass adjusted to the latitude, and a setting for the sun's "declination," or position each day as it varies from summer to winter, allowed the surveyor to find the true meridian. The solar compass revolutionized early land surveying and subdivisions by providing a true north-south direction.

The solar compass was so accurate that it was adopted by the federal government. In 1845 Burt carried out the nation's first combined linear-geological survey. (In 1849 Burt did not renew his patent on the solar compass on advice from the government, allowing it free use of his invention. He later regretted the decision because he never received adequate monetary compensation for his apparatus.) However, government officials did acknowledge Burt and his five surveyor sons as being among their most accurate surveyors.

Burt's other accomplishments included invention of the equatorial sextant in 1856 which aided maritime navigation. He also discovered iron ore near Marquette, Michigan, and pushed the state legislature to construct shipping locks at Sault Sainte Marie. Burt Lake, located near the northern tip of the Lower Peninsula, southwest of Cheboygan, was named after him.

Burt's Octagon in Mount Vernon is owned by Jean and Ira Holcomb; Ira is president of the Washington Historical Society. It has eight equal sides with an unusual second-story veranda that continues around all eight sides. The wood-frame clapboard house has decorated angular-scalloped barge boards on the first and second stories. Burt built other houses in Mount Vernon, three of which are known as "Burt Chalets," but this house was his only octagon.

Michigan is rich in extant octagons, due in part to the fact that Orson Fowler lectured in Marshall and Kalamazoo. Fowler left an indelible mark on Michigan and the Currier Octagon is one of the most unique.

Footnotes

1. Robert A. Schweitzer, "Octagon Houses," *Chronicle, The Quarterly magazine of the Historical Society of Michigan* (1981) 17.

2. Carl F. Schmidt and Philip Parr, *More About Octagons* (no publishing information available.)

3. Walter Creese, "Fowler and the Domestic Octagon," *Art Bulletin,* Vol. 28 (1946) 96.

4. Orson S. Fowler, *The Octagon House, A Home for All New York,* (N.Y. 1973) 5.

5. Ibid., 6.

6. Schweitzer, 19.

7. Virginia Bond, *"History of the Washington Octagon"* (1952)

8. "Octagon House as Alive Now as It Was in 1860," *The Macomb Daily* (Feb. 25, 1976), Section 4B.

9. Alan S. Brown, "William Austin Burt—A Pioneer Michigan Inventor," *Michigan Heritage,* Vol. 4, (Spring, 1963), 149–153.

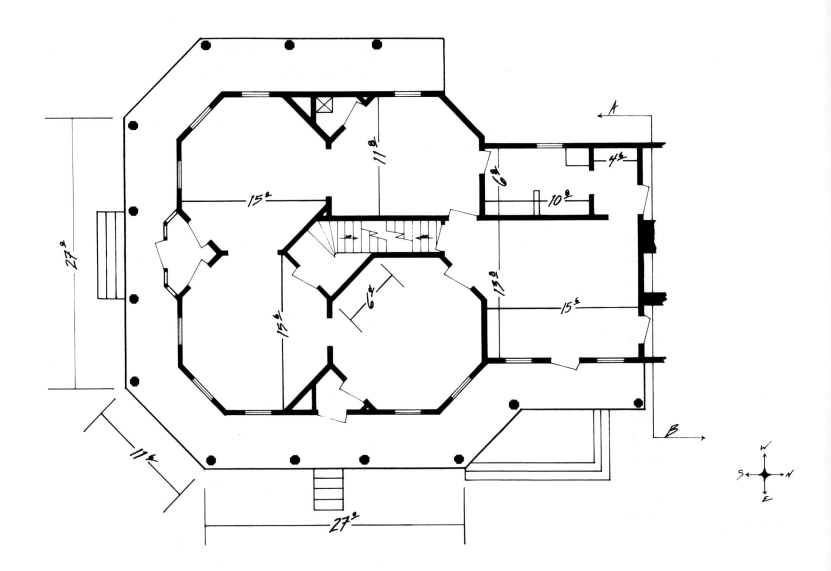

CHAPTER 4

The Currier Octagon, Its Plan and Construction

The Frederick P. Currier house is the only octagon in Almont and is a unique application of Orson Fowler's principles. It is located east of the Almont central business district at 231 East St. Clair Street in Section 22 of the Almont Township map.

It is highly likely that Currier learned of the octagon during his extensive business travels throughout southern Michigan. It's even possible that he heard Orson Fowler's lectures on the octagon in Kalamazoo or Marshall in 1850. In any case, the home certainly reflects the free-thinking spirit Currier expressed in his several business pursuits.

Currier was well versed in the carpentry and masonry trades, having constructed mills in Almont and Imlay and earlier in Vermont and Connecticut.

13. Currier Octagon first floor drawing
Frederick P. Currier I decided to build four perfect equal sided octagons on the main floor, making the four exterior sides longer than the four corners. The triangular shaped spaces created by joining the octagons are used as door entries or closets. A walk through this floor gives a better understanding of the light and beauty.

Early Michigan pioneers built their own homes or hired someone accomplished in the building trades to assist them. Hiring an architect specifically to design a residential home was not common in the mid-19th century, especially in a small town. It is quite possible, therefore, that Frederick P. Currier built his own home with assistance from local carpenters and masons.

Fowler's concept that "every man be his own builder" appealed to Currier and others who were struck by Fowler's freely eclecticized octagon designs. Few builders across the country adhered to all of Fowler's guidelines, adapting instead to the availability of materials, cost and individual tastes and needs regarding decor and interior space. Fowler's *Home For All* served as a guide to particular building techniques and aesthetic principles.

Currier's home is not a classic example of a Fowler Octagon. It is, however, a personal expression of the tastes of a successful businessman choosing the best of Fowler's suggestions to create a home well-suited to his personal and family needs.

Currier purchased the land for his octagon on January 4, 1849, from Calvin A. and Clarissa M. Shaw

14. Currier Octagon cellar

These oak beams in the cellar were hand hewn and show no signs of sagging after 141 years.

of Almont for $200. The property description in the deed reads: "Beginning 20 rods north of the southwest corner of the east half of the west half of the southwest quarter of Section 22."

This deed also includes "one other piece or parcel of land which now is used for a lane running from St. Clair Street north to the above-described land one rod in width lying on the east line of land owned and occupied by Mark Farley."

The exact date of the octagon's construction is not known, although it commonly is stated as 1854. It is quite possible that it was built earlier in view of the date of the land purchase. Currier and his family lived next door in the Bostick House at 235 East St. Clair Street until the octagon was completed.[1]

Had he built a house 15 years earlier, construction methods would have precluded Currier's choice of an octagon plan. Building techniques used in the Currier house reflected the latest in the evolving field of home construction. The earliest settlers built their houses of heavy timber frame construction, called post-and-girt. In this system, the weight of the second floor is supported by heavy corner posts and others widely spaced between the corners. Floor joists hung from the frame, unsupported below, making it difficult to place much weight on the second floor.

Availability of inexpensive wire nails and commercially sawn lumber led to a modification of the post-and-girt system in the early 19th century. Braced-frame construction consisted of a heavy timber frame with hewn joints and closely spaced vertical studs nailed between the horizontal timbers. Floors were supported by two-by-fours and internal walls thus became weight-bearing.

Balloon Framing

By the 1830s, another major change in building technology was introduced in Chicago. "Balloon framing" completely eliminated the need for massive timbers and hewn joints. Structures were built completely of two-by-twos, two-by-fours and two-by-sixes, as they are today. Two-by-fours extended a full two stories, and corner posts and horizontal members were two-by-fours nailed together. This allowed cheap and rapid construction and freed up the building form. Irregular shapes could be constructed with nails which helped eliminate the use of heavy timbers. The earlier timber-framing, however, was a sturdy building technique, and Currier incorporated three hand-hewn beams, still visible in the cellar, to support his two-story octagon of balloon frame construction.

The true craftsmanship of the masons is evident in the walls of the cellar foundation which are of cobblestone and fieldstone laid in regular courses one and one-half feet thick, consistently maintaining the octagon shape of the exterior (see figure 14). The above-ground foundation is laid in regular courses of cobblestone which were restabilized during the recent restoration.[2]

Over the balloon frame, Currier laid flush wide sawn boards in a horizontal configuration, which can be seen on the west facade of the house. This type of construction was a commonly-used alternative to clap-

board siding, although most of the exterior has clapboard siding.

Significant features of the octagon's exterior are the unequal wall lengths, the windows, porch and octagonal cupola. While an octagon is defined as "eight consecutive walls," nowhere in Fowler's book does it state that all eight sides must be of equal length. Currier opted for a modification; the four long walls are 20.5 feet in length, while the four shorter ones at the corners are six-feet long. Currier felt free to adapt the octagon to his liking.

Another unique feature, located beneath the junc-

15. Currier Octagon porch window
Long windows that extend to the floor of the porch give the house its' beautiful light.

ture of the roof with the house and extending as a band around the circumference of the house, is an unusually wide frieze board accentuating the prominent windows and octagon shape (see figure 15).

Fowler emphasized the use of tall windows in octagons because, he said, square and rectangular buildings created dark corners. Since tall windows let in more light, Fowler felt they provided a more healthy living environment. Currier's Octagon implements Fowler's window ideas; sash windows abound, six-over-six panes on the second floor and four-over-four on the first floor. The windows are consistently two feet, nine inches wide, and most of the panes are original. All of the windows are framed by tall shutters hanging on hinges, revealing their original utilitarian function. Inside, small metal wheels, located at the top of window frames, were probably added later to provide for a raising and lowering of shades. The small window on the west facade may have been added after the house was taken over by the Moses Alonzo Currier family. At that time, too, the small closet in the northwest interior octagon room

was made into a bathroom when Moses Jr.'s wife, Mary, could no longer climb stairs.

Two doors provided access into the octagon, a front door on the south facade and a side door on the east facade. Two metal boot scrapers remain in their original position on the porch at either side of the stairway leading to the side door. Transom lights are situated over both doors and oversized side-lights extending the full height of the first floor create a projecting front entrance bay. Smaller sidelights flank the six molded-panel front door which retains its original hardware (see figure 16).

A porch surrounds the octagon on five sides and extends slightly beyond the main core to the rear appendage on the first floor. It had deteriorated badly until Frederick P. Currier IV had the porch restored in 1987. Restoration was carried out according to late 19th century photographs showing its original condition. The porch roof was replaced at the same time with gray asphalt shingles to match the roof of the house. Below the porch roof line are decorative scrollwork brackets supporting the projecting cornice. Brackets are fixed to a front fascia board supported by 12 octagonal porch posts. Porch posts and brackets were taken to a millwright for an accurate match and reproduced with the same care that went into milling the originals. Porch posts are capped with curved octagonal capitals and supported by an octagonal base.

Long-lasting Wolmanized lumber was used for a new porch floor and the porch apron with inset lattice

16. Currier Octagon foyer
The front door opens into a small triangular foyer with one door facing into the main living room and the other into the parlor.

17. Currier Octagon post detail
The octagonal motif is carried over to the shaping of the posts, capitals and the base.

work, and front and side steps also were replaced. An upper hinged door on the east facade's northern end indicates a cool storage area where vegetables and other perishable foodstuff may have been kept.[3]

All in all, the porch reflects its former glory, a place where the Currier family enjoyed meals, afternoon teas and many a warm summer night.

An 1863 map of Lapeer County contains a lithograph of the Currier octagon featuring a wrought iron balustrade extending along the upper edge of the cupola as well as the main roof. An octagonal cupola perches on top of the house as a visual crest accentuated by 20 small frieze windows. A trap door in the roof of the cupola allows exterior access, probably for repairs and star gazing (see figure 18).

Although Fowler suggested the installation of cupolas and had a glass one installed atop his own octagon in Fishkill, New York, the concept was more likely transplanted from New England. Cupolas and "widows' walks" were common on coastal New England homes where, tradition holds, sailors' wives would pace the rooftops in endless search for husbands lost at sea.

Three chimneys project from the roof line, one each on the east and west facades and one at the junction of the main core and the addition. They accommodated iron stoves which were replacing fireplaces in the second quarter of the 19th century. Although Fowler recommended installing a centralized heating unit with a furnace in the basement, Currier chose to utilize individual room stoves instead of the newer heating technology. This reflected his interest in the foundry business. He probably designed and manufactured his own stoves at his foundry on North Main Street. It would be interesting to see what intricate designs Currier chose for his stoves, but nothing remains now except the flue openings in the walls. A chute for storage of coal is located in the garage, showing Currier's choice of heating methods.

Currier's deviation from Fowler's principles is evident in the interior floor plan. Entry is through a three-foot wide opening into a triangular vestibule with walls six feet in length. Fowler recommended this entry configuration to save heat since cold wind rushing in from an open door could be contained and not be allowed to travel throughout the rest of the house. He felt long, narrow passageways in square and rectangular house plans were a waste of space and socially inhibiting. Fowler also claimed the octagon plan made "entertaining handy where guests can go from room to room without going through a cold, wide entryway." He also stated that "the juxtaposition of rooms generally promotes sociability whereas the dividing entry partially breaks the spell."[4]

Fowler also felt the octagon plan was energy efficient because heat radiated from room to room rather than escaping through doors and wall partitions common in square and rectangular buildings. Actually that was a fallacy since there are more interior walls in octagons than in square or rectangular houses. Currier must have been aware of this since he made better use of the interior space with fewer wall partitions than the floor plans illustrated in Fowler's book. Currier's Octagon has a very wide-open, spacious feel, with high ceilings. He follows Fowler's premise here that the rooms are all united, "saving the housewife steps."[5]

Another departure from Fowler's suggested floor plans are three perfect octagon rooms on the first floor.[6] Fowler's interior floor plans actually exhibit few octagon shapes; he proposed using smaller square or rectangular rooms, resulting in additional wall partitions and more wasted, hard-to-use space than Currier's arrangement.

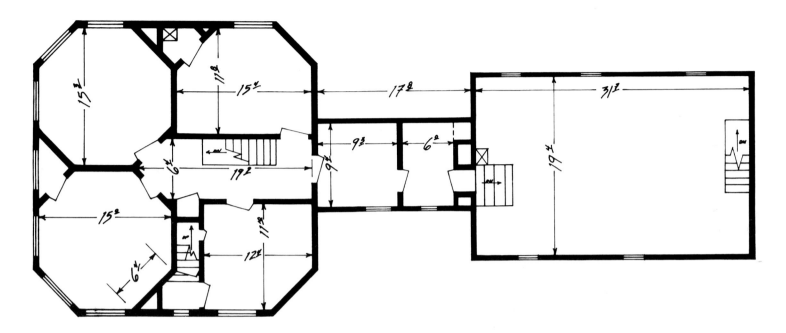

Four Unique Octagon Rooms

One of the most interesting architectural features of the Currier home is the fact that its four basic downstairs rooms are pure octagon-shaped (save for the one case where provision was made for a staircase). The theme is carried out on the second floor also.

Currier's configuration of large octagonal rooms leaves only three irregular spaces: a triangle closet between the northeast and southeast octagons, an irregular-shaped closet between the northwest and southeast octagons, and a small irregular-shaped area in the center of the house at the base of the stairway to the second floor. Currier's plan is actually superior to any of Fowler's plans in its efficient use of space.

Interior decorative features are equally impressive. The original oak, pine and butternut molding and trim can still be seen throughout the house (see figure 20). There are wide ceiling moldings in all four first floor rooms. An additional ceiling molding is located in the southwest and southeast rooms repeating the octagon shape. The original pine and butternut wainscoting on all eight walls of the northeast octagon suffered water damage during the William Hahns ownership (1961–1985) due to a leak in the ceiling (see figure 21). Restorationists have used numerous methods to remove the water stains, but to no avail. The pine flooring is in good condition and is sanded and refinished. Two sets of large doors once hung in the arched openings between the two south octagons and the northwest and southwest octagons. They were usually taken down during the summer months. One has been found and will be remounted.

---

18. Currier Octagon second floor drawing
On the second floor, space was taken from each of the back bedrooms for the stairway. The front southeast bedroom was the master bedroom, while the southwest bedroom was for the daughter. The two boys had the back two bedrooms. In the winter, family members could walk north through a long connecting room to a small set of stairs which put them over the interior toilet on the first floor.

Second Floor Plan

A straight, narrow stairway located at the center of the house provides access to the second floor. A turn to the right at the top of the stairs leads to a narrow 16-foot, five-inch-long hallway with a built-in closet on the east wall. The hall leads to the two front bedrooms. The southeast octagon contains a triangular opening on the south wall between the two octagons. Due to the layout of the southern octagon rooms, a window was never installed, creating an unbalanced appearance on the exterior facade. Frederick P. Currier IV remedied this situation by having the restorationists place a false window on the second floor, creating a symmetrical exterior fenestration.

The northeast bedroom has only five walls because of the need to accommodate a hallway. A two-feet, eight-inch-storage space on the south wall abuts the bottom riser of the staircase. The door on the south wall of the bedroom opens into a small space with a window on the east wall and a landing and staircase leading to the cupola. The cupola is octagonal in shape with walls of unequal length mirroring the octagonal plan of the house. The ceiling is not as high as the ceiling in the main house, and small frieze windows are located just below the roof line. Four windows are located on the four long walls and one window at the shorter walls, making a total of 20 windows.

Two openings at the southeast and southwest corners of the cupola lead to an attic space for the main house. It surrounds the cupola on all eight sides. The space never was used for living quarters due to the low slope of the roof, but it probably made a wonderful hiding place for children! The interior of the cupola was

---

18. Belvedere Cupola
This octagonal cupola has 20 small frieze windows which are better used for light than viewing.

used as a bedroom at one time and retains wallpaper and a calendar dating from the early 20th century.

The northwest bedroom has six walls; the long east wall is 15-feet, four-inches to provide for the staircase. The longer north and south walls are seven feet, nine inches and the shorter walls six feet, four inches. There is only one four-foot, seven-inch wide window in the bedroom, the same width as the other windows in the house. An irregular-shaped closet with five walls is located off the southwest corner of the room, from which point a chimney projects through the roof line.

On the second floor, at the rear of the addition, is a nine-foot, four-inch square bathroom with modern built-in bathtub and shower, toilet and sink. Originally the space probably was used for storage or a closet. The room most likely was not converted to a bathroom until well into the 20th century since Moses Alonzo Currier and his wife chiefly occupied the first floor. One window on the east wall is three-feet, 11-inches. The room north of the bathroom is 17-feet x 14-feet, seven-inches and has one three-foot, eight-inch wide window on the east wall. The room was paneled at some point and has recessed shelf space on the north wall. Philip Currier remembers a tank in this corner which held water pumped up from the cistern in the basement. This room now is used as storage space.

Four steps descend to the 31-foot, seven-inch x 19-foot, four-inch attic space above the wood and carriage sheds. The room has exposed rafters and could easily be utilized for living space if it were insulated and refinished. A staircase at its north end descends to the first floor hallway just outside the privy. In the winter one could stay inside and reach the three-hole facility from a long hallway on the west side and by the staircase from the second floor at the north end of the building.

An appendage at the rear of the house was added shortly after construction. Such additions were common in the 19th century as families grew and needed more space. The addition is also frame construction, covered with wood clap boarding. The north wall of the octagon and the second floor and west facade of the rear appendage have since been covered with aluminum siding. The placement of windows in the addition is not as symmetrical as the main octagon, reflecting the use of windows as utilitarian rather than decorative features. Two doors in the rear appendage serve as entrances into different functional living spaces.

The Kitchen, the Pantry and the Carriage Shed

The area directly north of the octagon on the first floor has always been used as a kitchen. The size of the stove, kitchen table, sink and cooking utensils necessitated a large kitchen space. Just west of the kitchen was a large pantry which was converted to a bathroom after the William Hahns purchased the home in 1961. The pantry held all the foodstuff and staples.

A smaller pantry located off the north kitchen wall probably held cleaning supplies, and another area north of the large pantry appears to have been used for washing. Water was pumped up from the basement cistern through two round holes in the floor. Remnants of this cistern are indicated by the raised concrete ledge

---

20. Currier Octagon ceiling molding

This molding may look like fine wood, but in most cases it is painted plaster which was discovered during the restoration work.

21. Dining room wainscoting

The pine and butternut wainscoting is used throughout the northeast octagon rooms including the dining room.

forming a holding area for water on the basement floor. Dirty wash water was probably thrown out the west wall window as there was not a plumbing system. An unusual winch located at the top opening of the door to the basement (in the garage) was used to lower barrels into the cellar. The long wooden cylinder with a rope attachment and iron crank handle are still visible.

The door on the north kitchen wall leads to a long narrow hallway which abruptly ends at a little room that is a remnant of a 19th century plumbing system—a three-hole "privy." The wooden ledge has been smoothed out after generations of use. Hallway walls were papered at some point to make the trip more pleasant.

A trap door on the interior wall north of the kitchen denotes the wood box. This feature saved walking outside on a cold, wintry morning to fetch wood. A room north of the kitchen was used as an area to chop wood. Philip Currier remembers many a cold winter day as a boy when his grandfather Moses chopped kindling to feed the wood stove in the kitchen where he often pensively sat and smoked his pipe.

The garage, or what used to be a carriage shed, has a 24-foot wide opening that accommodated large carriages and now is adequate for two contemporary mid-sized automobiles. A stairway at the rear leads to the floor above. Behind the carriage shed, a few steps down from the privy, is the work shed with its own entrance door. Three large eight-paned windows, two flanking the door and one small window on the north wall allow plenty of light.

Located to the northeast of the octagon at the end of the driveway is a one and one-half story, front-gabled board-and-batten barn. This was home for Currier's horses and a storage area for farming equipment. The west side of the barn contained a room for chickens and horse mangers. Philip Currier tore out

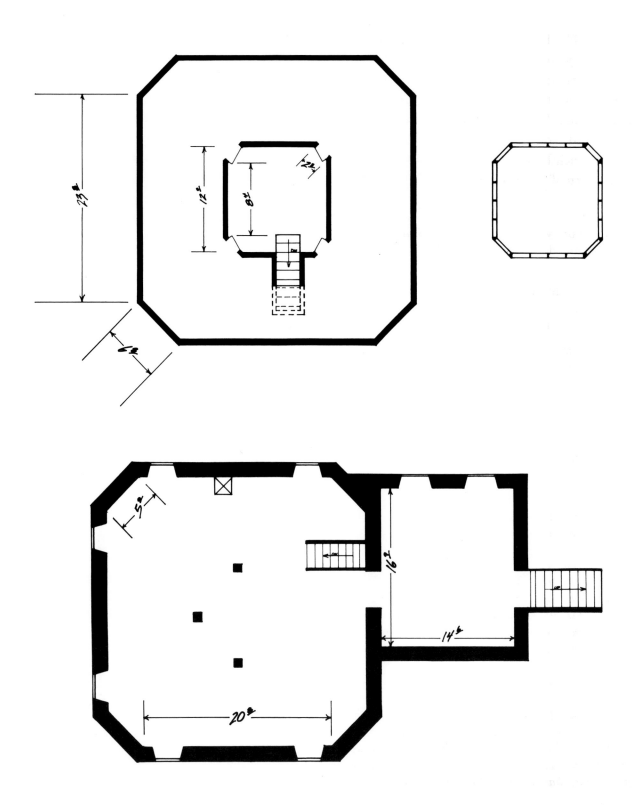

this interior.[7] The barn served a variety of purposes throughout the years.

The Currier octagon stands as a symbol of idealism, embodying a fever for experimentation and defense of the common man. The new philosophical trend was promoted by individuals like Orson Fowler and would flower in the social and economic Progressive movement at the turn of the century.

Footnotes

1. According to family lore, F.P. Currier paid his carpenters and masons $1.00 a day from sunrise to sunset, a standard rate at that time.

2. Although not visible on the south and east facades of the building due to the wooden lattice porch apron, the finely laid masonry work can be seen on the west facade.

3. Phil Currier remembers when this area served as a shelter for his grandfather Moses Alonzo Currier's dog.

4. Fowler, 99.

5. Ibid.

6. The northwest room has six walls instead of eight, the long straight wall necessary to accommodate the stairwell. The consistency in wall length illustrates the precision of builders.

7. The addition does not appear on the 1863 lithograph, indicating it was added later.

---

22. Architectural Drawing of Belvedere
This room on the top of the house has a mysterious feeling. One can look out in all directions with the 20 small windows, but you need to be over six feet tall, because of the height of the windows!

23. Architectural Drawing of Currier Octagon Basement
This basement consists of two large rooms which in the early years acted as a large storeroom for fruits and vegetables which was accessed by a large wooden slide located next to the stairs. The walls were made of fieldstone and an early type of grout which has lasted to the present time.

CHAPTER FIVE

The Currier Family and Almont

As the second half of the 19th century began, Frederick Plumer Currier, the transplanted New Englander, found himself well established in business and comfortably living with his family in a unique home.

Beyond that, he was poised to play an important role as Almont evolved into an active, thriving town and developed a diversified economy. Businesses multiplied, the population and manufacturing base expanded, roads improved, the railroad came to town, and educational efforts were refined.

Improved communication and transportation contributed to Almont's growth. Wooden-plank and packed-dirt roads criss-crossed the township, radiating outward and providing links with burgeoning Lower Peninsula communities. Built and maintained by farmers and property owners, the plank roads

24. Agricultural Works
This scene displaying the Currier Agricultural Work's finished products as well as the shop workers was photographed about 1870-75. The roller, hay rake, and plow were just a few of the implements produced by this thriving factory.

required financial support, and weary, frustrated travelers were all too happy to pay the 50-cent toll from Detroit to Almont. Toll gates located one mile north and one mile south of Almont stopped travelers in 1853.

To journey over Michigan's crude roads was dangerous and slow at best. Many a wagon wheel or horse's leg were broken or mired in the mud. Protruding tree trunks caused wagons to tip over, people and belongings spilling on the ground. Plank roads made the journey easier and towns that maintained a well-integrated system were more likely to attract newcomers. Almont Township used plank roads until 1870 when gravel roads began to appear.[1]

Another important link to the outside world was provided in 1852 when W.W. Maynard established the *Almont Palladium.* Maynard remained the *Palladium's* editor until it passed into the hands of Henry Ulrich and Peter Ferguson in 1854. They changed the name to *Almont Leader* and ran the paper until Ferguson's death in 1855. Ulrich then sold the *Leader* to George Brewster who successfully ran the paper until the *Almont Herald* was established by A.H. Patterson in January 1875. He continued to manage the *Herald* until 1881 when J.M. Johnson and his son succeeded him. Frank M. Johnson became the sole proprietor and editor on March 2, 1882. The paper continues to serve Almont's residents and surrounding communities as the *Tri-City Times,* now headquartered on South Main Street.

The newspaper carried much the same information and diversity of news as do contemporary papers, ranging from national and international updates to local "who's who" stories. Throughout the years, accounts of the Curriers' travels and social activities were frequently announced in the social column.

New businesses advertised their wares in the *Palladium.* The National Hotel (later called the

Herrington House) was built by Gary Goodrich in 1852 on the northwest corner of North Main and Saint Clair Streets. Its advertisements boasted of low rates and fine cooking. Other businesses rapidly expanded. In 1854 the McEntee Brothers established the manufacture of fanning mills. Joseph Simon started a carriage business in 1855 that became J. Simon and Son in 1857. William Morgan set up a livery business in 1856 and founded the firm of Gould, Morgan and Company. The present day Muir Brothers Funeral Home was formerly the location of L.M. Retherford's market where he practiced the butcher's trade in 1861. B.F. Johnston's furniture business opened in 1865.

Charles Ferguson and his Enterprises

The starch factory that Briggs and Teller purchased in 1851 was transferred to McHardy and Morton who ran it as a steam and grist mill between 1857 and 1858. Charles Ferguson, a prominent civic figure in Almont, then purchased the grist mill and operated it until 1862. Born in Scotland in 1822, Ferguson came to America in 1842 and married Charlotte McHardey of Aberdeen, Scotland, in Rust, New York, in 1846. They had three sons and one daughter. Ferguson and his family emigrated to Almont in 1848 and became involved in farming, general merchandising, mill operations and lumbering.

Census takers recorded valuable information which dramatizes the vast differences in costs of labor, materials and energy sources between the 19th century and the present. The 1860 census lists Ferguson's $1,000

25. Agricultural shop workers
Pictured here is the ten man work force of the Currier Agricultural Works, located on Main Street in Almont, Michigan. Standing on the far left is Rider, the manager. In total, this work force earned up to $350 per month.

investment in the lumber business. In that year he employed one male at $30 a month and sold 200,000 feet of lumber valued at $1,200. The $5,000 mill proved to be a more lucrative investment, yielding $23,000 in flour and $11,000 in meal and feed. Wheat cost one dollar a bushel and other grain cost 50 cents a bushel. The mill ran on steam and 25-horse power and employed three males at a total monthly labor cost of $100.

Currier's Agricultural Works

Frederick P. Currier's foundry represented a capital investment of $14,000, and the 1860 census showed him using 70 tons of pig iron valued at $23.10 a ton, 10 tons of wrought iron at $11 and 200 cords of wood valued at $250. He employed 10 men for a monthly labor cost of $350 and used steam power as well as 10-horse power. The foundry manufactured plows, threshing machines, gearing and two engines, a total value of $1,500.[2]

While Almont's businesses thrived, the outbreak of the Civil War prompted men all over the countryside to volunteer, leaving their comfortable lives and loving families to fight for their country. Michigan sent 90,000 men into battle. In 1864 Almont voted to levy a tax to pay $400 each to all persons volunteering for the army.[3]

Returning from the long, bloody war, soldiers found favorable conditions in Almont, and the decade of the 1870s proved to be a prosperous one. The township had a population of 2,298, 1,140 females and 1,158 males, and 462 families. There were 446 dwellings in addition to buildings for diversified industrial and agricultural works, grist mills, a sash, door and blind factory, a stave mill, wool carding mill and carriage shops.

The majority of industrial and commercial enterprises were located in the town of Almont. Lucrative farms scattered throughout Almont township supplemented the industrial economy by selling agricultural products to a larger market. Farmer, stock and "wool growers'" were Hiram Howland, District No. 3; William A. Matteson, District No. 3, and James McRoy, District No. 1.[4] James Riddle in Frac (Fractional) District No. 1 was a farmer and breeder of Durham cattle as well as being engaged in lumbering. Robert Steenson was a farmer and mason in District No. 8; W.S. Webster a farmer and proprietor of a grist mill in Frac District No. 2, and E.C. Bostick an "eclectic physician" in Frac District No. 4.

Some agricultural statistics from the 1870 census indicate the impact of farming in Almont Township:

1870 Census Data for Almont Township

$1,002,810	cash value of farms
13,084	acres of improved land
4,715	acres of woodland
2,633	acres of other improved land
$355,861	cash value of farming implements
$826,799	total wages paid, including board

ANIMALS

$146,133	value of livestock
$39,079	value of animals slaughtered or sold for slaughter
9,230	sheep
793	swine
778	other cattle
599	"milch cows"
600	horses
33	working oxen
4	mares and asses

PRODUCTS

$210,731	estimated value of all farm products including betterments and additions to stock

$9,900	orchard products
$2,155	forest products
66,205	pounds of butter
55,771	bushels of oats
44,062	bushels of winter wheat
34,725	bushels of Indian corn
33,461	pounds of wool
16,833	pounds of potatoes
13,385	pounds of cheese
10,230	pounds of hops
6,139	bushels of barley
3,178	tons of hay
2,914	bushels of spring wheat
335	bushels of buckwheat
40	bushels of cloverseed

A comparison between 1870 and 1874 figures demonstrates significant growth. The 1874 county census shows 21,836 acres of taxable land and 14,902 acres of improved land and production of 9,738 pounds of maple sugar and 306 barrels of cider.[5] A major increase from 1870 is noted in the amounts of butter, corn, other grain and "milch cows." Interestingly, the rural-urban conflict was evident even in those days. At a town meeting in 1860, for instance, the board approved a resolution stating that hogs were not allowed to run at large and that the board should provide for a pound.

While agriculture played a dominant role in the economic expansion of the township, F.P. Currier's foundry continued to increase its manufacture of stoves, plows and other farming implements. He decided to leave the foundry business to pursue other interests and sold Currier, Moses and Company to his son, Henry, in 1869. Born in Topsham, Vermont, April 23, 1840, Henry A. Currier was well-prepared to take over, having learned the machinists' trade in his father's shop at 16 years of age. He was married to Mary E. Charter of Northport, Michigan, on October 3, 1868. They had only one child, a daughter named Jenny.

Later Henry sold his interest in the company to his brother Frederick P. Jr., but he remained active patenting, improving and manufacturing farm implements for H.A. Currier & Bro. He invented the celebrated plows that bear his name and received patents on several inventions, including a cutter gear and sleigh runners.

According to family legend he had a total of 16 patents under his name.

Following is a list of implements manufactured by the Curriers:[6]

CURRIER NO. 1 PLOW (FIG. 26)
This plow took three first prizes at plowing matches for being the lightest of draft and the best general use plow. "One of the strongest iron beam plows," it turned a furrow from 11 to 15 inches wide.

CURRIER'S WHEEL CULTIVATOR
Manufactured since 1869, this six-tooth cultivator claimed to be a stronger, more durable general purpose cultivator than any on the market. It could be used to advantage in cultivating corn. The advertisement read, "Where a farmer had both a Currier and a foreign made cultivator. . . the old reliable Currier comes to the front, and in the language of many of our customers, 'It is the boss.'"

CURRIER NO. 2 PLOW (FIG. 27)
This wood beam plow was patented on November 9, 1890, and could be adjusted for two or more horses. It had handles that could be adjusted sideways or up and down. It was the cheapest plow on the market at that

6   CURRIERS' AGRICULTURAL WORKS,

CURRIER NO. 1 PLOW.

This Plow has been in the market for the past three years, and has given as good satisfaction for a General Purpose Plow as any Plow in the country. It has taken **Three First Prizes** at plowing matches over all competitors as being the lightest of draft and the best general use Plow. Is easily handled. Turns a furrow from 11 to 15 inches wide, and does its work well. It is one of the strongest Iron Beam Plows made, and well adapted to new or stony land. Sells upon its merits. Either Cast or Steel Mould Boards.

Price with Steel Mould Board, $................................

Price with Cast Mould Board, $................................

ALMONT, MICH.   5

CURRIER NO. 2 PLOW.

This Plow was introduced last season, and wherever used gave universal satisfaction. It is a wood beam Plow, and can be adjusted for two or more horses. The handles, by adjusting one bolt, can be moved up or down, or sidewise, to suit the purchaser. We claim it to be one of the very best Plows in Michigan. It holds easy, is very light in draft, and does as good work as any Plow made. Is equally as strong and weighs twenty pounds lighter than any other Plow we make, and is the cheapest Plow in the market. This is the only Plow on which "Currier's Patent Jointer" is used at present. Turns a furrow from 12 to 16 inches. Extra Cast or Steel Mould Boards furnished.

Price complete with Steel Mould Board, $................................

"   "   " Cast " , " $................................

time and 20 pounds lighter than any plow manufactured by H.A. Currier and Bro. It turned a furrow 12 to 16 inches wide.

CURRIER JOINTER NO. L
Originally made for the Currier No. l Plow, the steel or wrought iron jointer could be attached to any iron beam plow.

H.A. Currier and Bro. made improvements to the following implements:

HUNTINGTON OR SCOTCH IMPROVED PLOW
A new landside, two new points and alterations strengthened this plow and made it more adaptable to heavy soils. The Curriers made available long or short handles.

FIELD ROLLER
The Curriers introduced this field roller with cast iron drums and kiln-dried white oak staves to Michigan in 1874. They made an improved spring seat and seasoned white oak or ash frame.

CURRIER IMPROVED SCOTCH HARROW
Improvements in this harrow consisted of hinges or couplings holding the harrow together in two or three sections, making it easier to tighten in case of timber shrinkage. The Improved Harrow took two first prizes at a Michigan State Fair.

---

26. Currier Plow No. 1
This prize winning plow was introduced in 1875

27. Currier Plow No. 2
Introduced in 1890, this plow was considered the latest improved model.

CURRIER IMPROVED TILL CULTIVATOR
This implement was improved to do the work of a cultivator and a hoe at the same time. It could be adjusted to throw soil to or from the rows by changing the two back teeth. The depth and width of blades could be adjusted also.

IMPROVED CHAMPION FEED CUTTER
This was awarded the International Medal at Buffalo, New York. It was capable of cutting one ton of feed per hour at different lengths. It also was capable of threshing peas.

IMPROVED FEED CUTTER
The revolving knife allowed cutting of wet or dry corn stalks. The machine combined strength, simplicity and utility to perform work simply and rapidly.

Other diverse implements manufactured by H.A. Currier & Bro. included cast iron kettles; cider; wine and jack screws; road scrapers; lever feed cutters; horse powers and jacks; winged and common shovel plows; cultivators; cutting boxes; corn shelters; gang plows; circular and drag wood-sawing machines; spring and diamond-tooth harrows; and iron and brass castings.

H.A. Currier & Bro. introduced the Peerless Plow in 1875. It took first prize that year at the "Union Farmers' Club" plowing match for lightness of draft over nearly all the leading plows on the market. H.A. Currier & Bro. sustained success until Henry's untimely death at 49 on May 28, 1889, from cirrhosis of the liver. He and his wife Mary are buried together in the Almont Cemetery. The foundry was sold on July 1, 1890, to R.E. Lee who continued to manufacture the Peerless Plow and land roller.

Currier and Townsend found the First Bank
After selling the foundry to Henry, the elder Frederick P. Currier invested $30,000 with Uriel Townsend to establish Almont's first bank in 1870. The Townsend and Currier bank was located on the northeast corner of North Main and St. Clair Streets. Born in New York in 1829, Uriel Townsend came to Michigan in 1834 and lived on a farm in Metamora. Townsend built his Gothic Revival home in 1865. This elegant home with Italianate brackets and projecting bay windows can be seen today at 315 West St. Clair in the historic district.

The bank attained a level of success, reflected in the 1884 History of Lapeer County which made this statement about the Currier and Townsend bank: "The confidence reposed in the bank by its patrons and the community generally is evidence that its business has been conducted with shrewdness, honesty and faithfulness to trust. A successful business has been the necessary result."

Despite this success, Townsend and Currier decided to seek other entrepreneurial pursuits. On December 2, 1872, they sold the bank for $60,000 to Charles Ferguson and his son, Charles R. Ferguson.[7]

Truly humanitarian and civic-minded, Ferguson held many offices in town. His name is repeatedly found in the court records associated with community functions. Ferguson & Sons was Almont's only bank until 1909 when Almont Savings Bank was organized. Ferguson's bank closed in 1921 due to financial difficulties.

---

28. Currier and Bro. farm tool catalogue
This H. A. Currier and Bro. brochure listed the main tools for sale and their prices in very calm yet boastful prose

29. Terry House
This house was built by Graham Terry in 1887 and is a strong example of the architectural quality found in the West St. Clair historical district. Randy and Wendy Eastman are the present owners. The house is located at 210 West St. Clair, just across from the town library.

In 1895, at the height of the bank's success, Charles Ferguson, Sr., built his spacious Queen Anne house at 306 West St. Clair Street. The opulent home with a large corner turret, and palladian and oculus windows is located in the West St. Clair Historic District. (See figure 30.)

After selling the bank, Currier and Townsend invested $75,000 with Henry Stephens and J.S. Johnson in a tract eight miles northwest of the city of Lapeer extending to Fish Lake. Currier and Townsend made healthy profits from lumbering. Currier began to speculate in real estate and owned property in Lapeer, St. Clair, and Sanilac counties, as well as property in the village. On July 30, 1878, M.T. Moore, Frederick P. Currier, Charles Ferguson, I.T. Beach and

W.W. Taylor donated a large plot of land to the town of Almont in appreciation for its support.

These men stated, "We do hereby dedicate to the public all streets represented thereon, and we do acknowledge said map as our legal subdivision of said

---

30. Ferguson House
This house was built by Charles Ferguson in 1895 and is typical of the style of the times with its asymmetrical composition. Queen Anne houses have a great variety of shapes and textures, as shown in the shingled and horizontal siding clad walls with octagon shingles in the gable ends. Also featured are the stained and leaded Queen Anne windows and oulus or "bulls-eye", and a palladian window on the east gable. This house is presently owned by Roger and Christine Bailey and is located at 306 West St. Clair.

land to be known as 'Moore's Addition of Almont.'" "Moore's Addition" included the southeast corner of the west quarter of the southwest quarter of Section 22, north of the Currier octagon.

---

31. Mackinac vacation

This scene of FPC I, his sons and son in law was taken in the 1870s when the Agricultural Works and his banking interests were at their peak. This group had traveled from Almont to vacation at the base of one of the historic rocky lookouts on Mackinac Island. FPC I is shown standing with a long coat and to his right is his son in law William Ovens. The two seated people just in front of the tent are FPC II (left) and his brother Henry (right).

Railroad Comes to Almont

A great benefactor to the town of Almont, Currier became a member of the Republican Party and regarded himself as a small-town aristocrat. One of his major contributions came in 1870 when the town voted to spend $45,000 for the construction of a railroad from Romeo to Almont. Currier donated the money for the Port Huron and Northwest Railroad which connected Almont with Port Huron and was completed in 1882.

The train ran a passenger service and provided freight cars for produce and livestock that aided in the development of the agricultural Thumb area of Michigan. R.K. Farnum built and owned a grain elevator at the Almont station of the Port Huron and

Northwest Railroad which flourished, reached a peak in 1900, and finally was abandoned in 1942.[8]

Series of Fires Destroy Downtown Almont

Other community services were established at this time. Several major fires provided the impetus for establishment of an Almont fire department: The first large fire in 1859 burned a hotel and two stores on the northwest corner of Main and St. Clair streets; the fire of 1861 burned all the buildings on the west side of South Main Street except a store on the southwest corner of Main and St. Clair streets; an 1866 fire burned five stores on the west side of South Main Street, and six buildings on the west side of North Main Street burned in 1867.

A Water Works Committee was formed in June 1878 and citizens voted to spend $2,000 to complete the well construction. In 1879 Currier sold a parcel of land on the west side of Main Street as the site for a building to house the fire engines. Currier stated that he would accept payment in taxes over the following years. The town completed the building on October 5, 1880, for $150, and on August 2, 1881, the pump was placed in the well that was dug in 1877 at the east end of Centennial Street. The town elected two fire wardens, one for the north district and one for the south. Their responsibilities included inspecting stove pipes for defects.

Another terrible fire on December 9, 1881, burned the Union School. The large two-story Classical brick structure had been built in 1867 from plans drawn by G.W. Lloyd. The town organized a committee in 1882 to plan for construction of a new schoolhouse. It was completed in April 1884. In the winter of 1894 another fire destroyed 10 buildings on the west side of South Main Street, one of which had been owned and used by the elder Currier.

FPC I Endures Both Family Deaths and Business Losses During his 70s and 80s

Every life has cycles, and that was true of Frederick P. Currier I's life. A low point for him was undoubtedly a four-year period between 1886 and 1894 when he was buffeted by a number of profound changes. His daughter and youngest son moved away from the family home in Almont to adjoining farms in Yale, Michigan, some fifty miles northeast of Almont. Three years later, first his eldest son, Henry, and then his wife, Mary, died. A year later, his foundry was sold, and his two brothers died—Moses in 1883 and Richard in 1894. All these events were followed hard by the Panic of 1893 when his financial foundation was severely affected.

However, some good news balanced the bad news, as often happens. A grandson, Frederick P. Currier III, was born in Yale in 1888 giving FPC I a total of four grandchildren. In 1896 the elder Currier re-married, taking as his bride, Mahala Currier, the widow of his brother, Moses. Clearly, however, Frederick P. Currier I was feeling the affects of a long and varied life during these years. He was 77 years old when his son Henry died, and according to news reports of the time he was allegedly too "feeble" to continue to run the foundry he and his son had managed, and he was forced to sell it. Yet there must have been some spark left because he continued to be an important figure in Almont's business.

That status is reflected in the following excerpt from the "Portrait and Biographical Record of Genesse, Lapeer and Counties", published in 1892.

"Frederick Plumer Currier is a capitalist residing in Almont. He was born in the township of Newbury, Orange County, Vermont, November 11, 1812, and is the son of Moses and Mary (Carter) Currier. Our sub-

ject began for himself at the age of nineteen years, work-ing out by the month for a time. He later attended the Newbury Seminary, and was also a student at Adkinson Seminary, New Hampshire. He learned the

32. FPC I in his prime
This photo of FPC I was taken in his prime during the 1870's.

33. FPC I's wife Mary Clark Currier
This is the only known image of FPC I's wife, Mary Clark (1813–1889) which was taken when she was in her seventies.

carpenters and joiners trade and followed that for a long time. From the age of twenty-one to twenty-five our subject lived at Haverhill, Massachusetts, and while there learned the shoe maker's trade, devoting himself to this during the winter months and thus became an expert workman and soon extended his effort in this direction by having a number of skilled workmen and running a shop of his own. During the summer he devoted himself to the work of masonry.

Our subject returned to Newberry and went into partnership with a Mr. Keys for the manufacture of *brick. He was married at the age of thirty-five on November 7, 1837, to Miss Mary P. Clark. Later our subject went to Topsham and in partnership with his brother built a large tannery, afterward selling out his interest to his brother. He then engaged in farming for one year and then returned to Vermont and from there to Connecticut and was variously engaged, part of the time in a paper mill and part time in building. In 1846 Mr. Currier came back to Michigan and built a large starch mill for the manufacture of starch from potatoes. He brought his family here in 1847, and from that time until 1851 he engaged in building mills. He then became interested in the furnace and machine business, which he followed in company with various parties until 1869. He was the principal one in the enterprise and furnished the greater part of the capital. He later withdrew from these various undertakings and started a bank under the firm name, Currier and Townsend, putting in $30,000 with Messrs. Johnson, Stephen, Townsend and Co. and in less than two years sold out for $60,000. He then began to speculate in real estate, in which he is still interested.*

Our subject has only two children now living although he has been the father of four. One died in infancy; one, Henry, was in the flower of his manhood when he died. His surviving son Frederick P. Currier, Jr., lives in St. Clair County; daughter Sarah married Wm. Ovens and lives in Yale, St. Clair County. Our subject has given to each of his children $12,000 in lands, money and machinery. He is a Republican in politics and has been appointed to various public offices and is a generous upholder of all enterprises and promises to be for the advantage of the locality. He is a member of and a Deacon in the Congregational Church. After the death of his first wife our subject married his brother's widow, Mahala Currier nee Doe."

The Currier family records include Frederick P. Currier's own draft copy of this text and it shows his own corrections of two items, namely the correct spelling of his middle name, Plumer, from the erroneous "Plumell" and the spelling of his wife's name as Mahala, not "Malahal" as it was initially written. [9]

In spite of these many problems Currier continued to play a vital role in Almont's growth. The fires did not affect Almont's growth, however. Population of the township went from 888 in 1840 to 2,050 in 1880. The value of Almont's real and personal property in 1882 reached $1,314,000, higher than any township in Lapeer County at that time. The value of forest products increased from $2,155 in 1870 to $8,748 in 1883. [10]

As the town increased its civic functions, Currier donated village lots numbered 105 and 106 to be used as the site of a town hall. William Myers was awarded the contract for $4,800, and the building was completed on March 6, 1884. Almont's town hall housed the council room, engine room, jail and town offices. It also was used for a variety of functions, such as rehearsals, traveling shows and dances. It also housed the fire department for many years. Deterioration and enormous maintenance costs led to Almont's regrettable decision to tear the building down in May 1987.

The 20th Century Brought the Automobile Revolution.

Automobile manufacturing plants were located in major urban centers such as Detroit, Pontiac and Flint, but foundries that produced agricultural implements for rural markets were also converted to auto parts fac-

---

34. FPC I in his later years.
This picture of FPC I was done in the 1890's when he was over 80 years old. The fact that he is holding his left hand suggests that he may have had a mild stroke. When his son Henry died in 1889, FPC I was considered "too feeble" to run the foundry, and was forced to sell it.

tories.[11] Ironically, Almont's population stabilized while the state boomed, because people stayed in the larger urban areas where the automobile jobs were.

Almont was affected by the automobile industry, nonetheless. In 1917 Charles Ferguson and several local businessmen bought H.A. Currier & Bro. Manufacturing Company from Cork Bros. and renamed it Almont Manufacturing Company.[12] They manufactured sleighs, cutters, plows, guns and rollers, products that had been introduced and marketed by H.A. Currier and Bro. Almont Manufacturing Company opened a second foundry in Imlay City by purchasing Hurd Lock and Manufacturing Company, a Detroit firm established in 1921. In 1931 the plant moved to Almont into the old H.A. Currier & Bro. foundry building on the corner of North Main and School Streets in Almont, and began the manufacture of automotive locks and molding. In 1936 Almont Manufacturing Co. changed its name to Hurd Lock and Manufacturing Co. A second plant opened in 1937 in Adrian to manufacture a line of automotive hardware and molding. The Almont plant continued to produce automotive locks for a national market under the name of Hurd Lock and Manufacturing Company.

After the Second World War broke out, the Navy awarded a contract to Hurd to produce ammunition components. Both the Adrian and Almont plants remained busy under this contract. In 1944, the company was awarded the Navy "E" for excellence in producing war materials. It also received the United States Treasury Minute Man flag because 90 percent of its employees purchased War Bonds on a payroll deduction basis.

The company resumed manufacture of automotive locks and hardware when the war ended in 1945. In 1957 Almont Manufacturing sold its interests in Hurd Lock Company to Avis Industries which continued to operate Hurd Lock until 1962 when it moved to Greenville, Tennessee. Hydraulic Tubes and Fittings, Inc., produced automotive parts in the building, now called the Lumberstore.

The fact that many Almont residents worked at auto plants in Detroit, Flint, and Pontiac, led to a new form of mass transportation—the electric interurban train. Almont residents donated money and land for the right-of-way. The first car arrived in Almont from Detroit on July 1, 1914. The Detroit United Railway (D.U.R.) track ran through Almont west of Main Street, following M-53 to Imlay City. It transported passengers and goods.

Detroit Edison provided electricity to Almont through electric lines on the Detroit and Northern Railroad right-of-way. In 1914 Detroit Edison purchased Frank Bishop's electric plant in Almont. The village voted in 1915 to give Detroit Edison a franchise.

Drop off and pick up points for the D.U.R. were located in the front room of the town hall and later in a house on West St. Clair Street. Popularity of the electric train faded with the increase in the number of individually-owned automobiles. Greyhound bus service began in 1925, transporting passengers from Imlay City to Detroit through Almont.

Changing modes of transportation led to an improved system of roads. Horatio S. Earle, a Michigan resident and proponent of transportation improvements, urged the state to participate in the construction of public roads. His persistence paid off, and he was named Michigan's first state highway commissioner, serving in office from 1905–1909.

Charles Scully, state senator from Almont, secured legislation for construction of M-53.[13] The southern end of M-53 began north of Detroit and continued out Van Dyke Avenue. It was named the "Earle Memorial Super Highway" in honor of Horatio S. Earle. The road extends through Romeo, Almont and Imlay City, north to Port Austin. Three stone monuments were erected in Earle's honor, one in Mackinaw City, one in Cass and a third in Almont. Dedicated on August 21, 1930, the Almont monument bears the names of the seven counties served by the Earle Memorial Super Highway.

Social improvements in the field of health care marked Almont's progressive attitudes in the 20th century. The Burley Hospital took care of the community's health concerns. Dr. David Burley began his medical career in Almont in 1893, and he continued to practice until his death in 1957. Born in Ontario on October 16, 1863, he received his medical degree from the Detroit College of Medicine. He opened Almont's first hospital around the turn of the century with his brother, Dr. Jacob Burley. Burley Hospital was located in the building that is now Muir Bros. Funeral Home on the southwest corner of Main and Mill Streets. The building was known as Hotel Almont before Burley occupied it. When William Hahn—who had purchased the Currier Octagon house in 1961—died in 1985, he willed some adjacent property to the Almont Hospital. John Bishop, Almont hospital administrator, subsequently sold some of the land.

Footnotes

1. See chapter II for a further description of road construction.

2. The 1860 census listed these as the products manufactured at Currier's foundry in that year.

3. Those individuals drafted also received $400.

4. A wool grower referred to one who raised sheep for yield of high-quality wool.

5. Between 1870 and 1874 there was an increase of 1,818 acres of improved land.

6. These implements were advertised in the *H.A. Currier & Bro. Manufacturers Illustrated Catalogue of Farm Tools,* ca. 1880.

7. The younger Ferguson was born in New York and received his education at a seminary in Ypsilanti, Michigan. He married Jennie M. Fatin of Hackensack, N.J., in 1871.

8. In 1870, Farnum had opened a sash, door and blind factory as well as maintaining a saw and flour mill.

9. The name "Plumer" has come down through the generations of Curriers. It was the last name of a preacher whose sermons must have impressed the Curriers to such an extent that they "adopted" the name. According to family legend, the Reverend Plumer allegedly uttered the notable phrase, "America was like a fire burning on top of a mountain" in one of his sermons in approximately 1775–1800. Philip Currier, the national genealogist of the Currier family located in Henniker, New Hampshire, has suggested that the Plumer name may have been the name of a family friend or a Currier wife in the 1775–90 period.

10. F.P. Currier served as the town assessor in 1883.

11. Sarah Ward Eubanks, Regional Planner, National Register Nomination, West St. Clair Historic District, 1986.

12. Lee Cork purchased H. A. Currier & Bro. from R.E. Lee in 1915.

13. Hildamae Waltz Bowman, Almont, *The Tale of Then and Now* (1985), 37.

CHAPTER SIX

The Twentieth Century

For Frederick Plumer Currier there seemed to be no end to the scope of his pioneering spirit. Most dramatic, of course, was the transition he made from the relatively urbane life of an Easterner to that of one carving out a living for his family in a midwestern wilderness. His success as business and family man was impressive.

By the 1880s, as noted, he had been involved in a variety of entrepreneurial efforts in Almont. Around 1885, the focus shifted to the community of Yale, a settlement just a few miles away. Currier had purchased land in the area. Now he would give each of his children 160-240 acres of farmland.

For Henry, who had taken over his father's foundry in 1869, the beneficence was short-lived. He was 49 when he died in May 1889.

Frederick Plumer Currier Jr. took up residence on

35. *Lake Huron*
This scene captured by Lewis Fitch after 1895 shows (from left to right) a young FPC III, Mayme Currier and Sarah (Currier) Ovens enjoying a sandy beach north of Port Huron.

his farm in 1885 and raised Holsteins. On July 28, 1887, he married Abigail Spring who was born in a small village (Whitchurch) north of Toronto. Her ancestors were from Tennessee and were of Quaker stock. Frederick Jr. and Abigail had two children, Frederick Plumer III born in January 1888 and Mary, or "Mayme" as she was affectionately called, born in 1886.

The senior Currier's third sibling, Sarah, was born in Topsham on December 26, 1843. In August 1882 Sarah married William Ovens, a native of Scotland, who ran a general store in Almont with his brother James from 1867 to 1883. The store carried the largest stock of general merchandise of any mercantile center north of Detroit. Records indicate the store shipped four and a half tons of butter to Detroit in one week in August 1879.

William Ovens worked for the lumberman Henry Stephens before opening his store. In 1889 William, Sarah and their son moved to the family farm in Yale. Ovens also ran a general store in Yale, established in 1866 under the name of Ovens and Braidwood.

Over the years, Sarah befriended Lewis Fitch who became the family photographer from 1895–1900, attending picnics and family outings on the Currier family farm in Yale. His animated, humanistic photographs depict friends and Currier family members in relaxed natural settings. The unusually candid portraits are in sharp contrast to the typical restraint of the late 19th century images.

---

36 Camping along Mill Creek
This image was taken by Lewis Fitch in about 1895-98 when he visited Sarah Ovens (fifth from left) and other friends in Yale, Michigan. Shown third from left is Mayme, her brother FPC III (sixth from left) and FPC II seated to left of the flag pole.

Fitch was an accomplished jeweler, silversmith and watch repairman, skills that were valuable to a photographer who profited from manual dexterity and fine detailed work. Fitch served with the Fifth Michigan Cavalry in the Civil War for three years. His friendship with Sarah produced many photographs of her enjoying picnics and wading in streams. William Ovens died in 1911 of a paralytic stroke. Fitch died in 1918. His obituary said, "He was very emphatic in likes and dislikes."

Frederick P. Currier I died in Almont on May 6, 1900. He and Mary are buried in Almont Cemetery. (After his wife's death in 1889, Currier married his brother's widow, Mahala Doe, the same year.)

Sarah wrote a tender letter to her brother, Frederick Jr., during her mother's (Mary) illness from injuries suffered in a fall. She had been up all night crying ("wiggened up") nursing her mother when she wrote: "She was so good to everyone near her who had an ill or an ache. She never had a cross word for us in her life." She died on January 25, 1889.

Shortly after Currier's death, the octagon house was taken over by Moses Alonzo Currier, son of his brother Moses. Young Moses was born September 21, 1861. He married Mary Emma Sawyer, and they lived in North Dakota before rejoining his mother, Mahala Doe, who had married his uncle Frederick. The young people ran a general store in Almont, then moved to Capac where they ran a store for 23 years.

They returned to Almont and lived in the octagon until Moses' death on September 10, 1935, after an eight-day illness. His friends spoke kindly of him: "Honesty of character and kindly, sympathetic ways won him respect and esteem of all who knew him." His wife Mary resided in the octagon until her death on December 3, 1960.

Moses Alonzo and Mary had two children, Frederick

Hale and Cecil Madeline Spencer. Born December 19, 1894, Hale Currier played on Almont High School's football team. He served as a sergeant in France during World War I and later assumed the responsibility of running his father's general store in Capac. He married Lucy Mellen Letts, granddaughter of Richard Mellen, William Austin Burt's associate.

On October 17, 1948, Frederick Hale Currier (see figure 43) mysteriously disappeared on a hunting trip in Newbury. He left his friends in the hunting lodge at dusk to hunt partridges. By the time they realized he was missing, a light snowfall covered the ground, obliterating potential evidence. Two hundred friends, neighbors, relatives and members of the football team made an exhaustive search of a 360-square mile area. The fact that he had not built a fire concerned them. When asked why so many searched for him, his friends responded: "Well, he's had the store (in Capac) for 30 years. His father was there before him and I guess—well, we just think a lot of him."[1] He was never found. A tombstone for Hale Currier was erected in Almont Cemetery next to other family members.

Hale and Lucy's sons were both born in Capac. James Currier, born September 29, 1926, was married to Ruth Olson June 27, 1951. He is a dentist. Philip Hale, born January 19, 1923, married Doris Meunier on June 27, 1946, on his grandmother Mary's 80th birthday. Philip worked for the Michigan State Liquor Control Commission. They both have children and grandchildren.

The son of Frederick Jr. and Abigail Currier, Frederick III, was born January 12, 1888 in Yale, attended public schools there and was graduated from Yale High School in 1906. He earned a teaching degree in 1909 from one of the finest teachers' colleges in the country, Michigan State Normal School in Ypsilanti (now Eastern Michigan University). In 1922, he married Margaret Hoedemaker, of Charlotte, Michigan.

Frederick P. Currier III became a successful athlete at Michigan Normal School. He was a baseball pitcher and shortstop and a center in basketball. Currier's avid interest in sports carried through to his teaching days. He taught math and coached basketball and baseball for two years at Alma High School. The school's 1911 yearbook noted that Currier's good coaching was responsible for producing winning teams in basketball and baseball.

Currier had dreamed of becoming a doctor, inspired by Dr. Watson of the Sherlock Holmes literary series. In 1913 he confidently walked up to the doors of the medical school of the University of Michigan in Ann Arbor and was accepted. He graduated with honors in 1916 and became the first intern at Blodgett Hospital in Grand Rapids after that institution had asked the medical school to send its best student. He later had two years of post-graduate study in Ann Arbor and one year in London.

Currier was a resident in medicine at the University of Michigan when the U.S. entered World War I. He volunteered, joined the Blodgett Hospital Unit (Unit Q) and mended wounded soldiers in a hospital in Paris in 1918 and 1919. He returned to Grand Rapids and spent some time in internal medicine with a Dr. Whinnery. He returned to the University for a year of neurology and psychiatry and then returned to Grand Rapids.

Currier conducted some of the country's earliest research on neurology. In 1931 he published an article

---

37. Picnic
From left to right, Sarah Ovens, Lewis Fitch, FPC III and Mayme Currier having lunch on the side of the road. This image was taken by Currier Ovens who was one year older than FPC III, shown here making faces at the photographer.

in a medical journal addressing forced grasping in the upper extremities as neurological evidence of a lesion of the opposite frontal lobe. This led him to work with the delicate intricacies and complex structure of the human brain. No doctors in the Grand Rapids area wanted to become involved with psychiatry, so Dr. Currier accepted the challenge and established the first psychiatric practice in western Michigan. In the early 1930s Currier worked with city health officials to establish sex education at Grand Rapids high schools.

Dr. and Mrs. Currier had three children. Frederick P. Currier IV now maintains dual residency in Detroit and San Francisco. Dr. Robert Currier is the Emeritus Chairman of the Neurology Department at the University of Mississippi Medical Center in Jackson, Mississippi. He is a nationally recognized expert on multiple scerlosis and ataxia, and has discovered some of the basic causes of these diseases. He married Marilyn Johnson in 1951. Suzanne Shaker, married to Webster Shaker on February 25, 1950, now lives in Evanston, Illinois. They all have children and grandchildren. Webster Shaker, now retired, was the Chairman and CEO of a large national representative firm, Elias Shaker & Co., which he headed for over 30 years.

Frederick P. Currier IV was chairman and chief executive officer of Market Opinion Research, headquartered in Detroit, Michigan. He received his M.A. in economics at the University of Illinois and finished Ph.D. course work in economics at the University of Chicago. He became chairman and CEO of Market Opinion Research in 1979. Market Opinion Research, one of the 25 largest survey research firms in the United States, handled polling for the last three Republican presidents of the United States.

Currier pioneered new methods of market segmentation, the ticket-splitter concept of political behavior and various aspects of media measurement. He was an adjunct professor of journalism, University of Michigan, where he taught economics of media.

Currier has three children by his first wife, Caroline Musselman, whom he married July 14, 1951. He now is married to Amy McCombs who works and lives in San Francisco. They were married July 10, 1986.

Nearly 150 years of Currier tradition and stories are told through the Almont Octagon. Thanks to Frederick Currier IV's care, patience and generosity, the Currier heritage will be kept alive for many generations to come.

Footnotes
1. This information comes from 1948 newspaper clippings covering the disappearance. The clippings are located in the Almont Library in a scrapbook of local history.

---

38. The Red House Farm
This farm was given to FPC II by his father and is located north west of Yale, Michigan, and as one can see it was a rather large establishment in terms of buildings with horse and hay barns. Mill Creek ran along a part of the farm, about 1/4 mile behind the windmill.

39. FPC II and his children
This remarkable shot by Lewis Fitch in 1899 shows FPC III at eleven years of age, his father FPC II and Mayme at 13.

40. *Mayme Currier (left) and her mother Abigail Currier (right) are shown in front of their home with an unidentified group of children in Yale, Michigan.*

41. The Currier Machine Shop interior in Yale, Michigan

The steam engine to the left was the main power source for this shop. The repair and maintenance of farm machinery and the woolen mill production line kept FPC II's shop busy.

42. Yale across the field

In this image, Lewis Fitch tried to capture the landscape of the small town across the farm fields, yet due to the limitations of photography in the 1890s, he was unable to accurately record the picture he could see.

43. Hale Currier, pictured here in his World War I uniform.
He ran the Capac General Store for 30 years before disappearing on a hunting trip. He was never found.

44. Capac General Store (1910-20)
This store was run by the Moses Currier family for over 40 years. A typical interior of a general store in small town Michigan.

45. A Joyous Christmas in the Currier Octagon house, 1950
Back row from left: Doris Currier, Philip Currier, Lucy Currier. Front row from left: George Anderson, May E. Currier, James Currier. (Refer to Moses geneaology chart)

46. World War I Medical Officers
This group of medical officers from Grand Rapids, Michigan, are shown during World War I in Paris where they ran a large hospital. Captain Frederick P. Currier III is shown seated in the front row on left.

47. Three Generations of Curriers
Dr. FPC III with his new born son FPC IV and his father FPC II on the front porch of their house in Grand Rapids, Michigan, in 1924.

48. Moses Currier genealogy chart
The Moses Currier line has produced 18 members both alive and dead. This family owned the Currier Octagon for 61 years and preserved the house in excellent condition. Currently, as in the FPC II line, their are no male heirs in the modern generation.

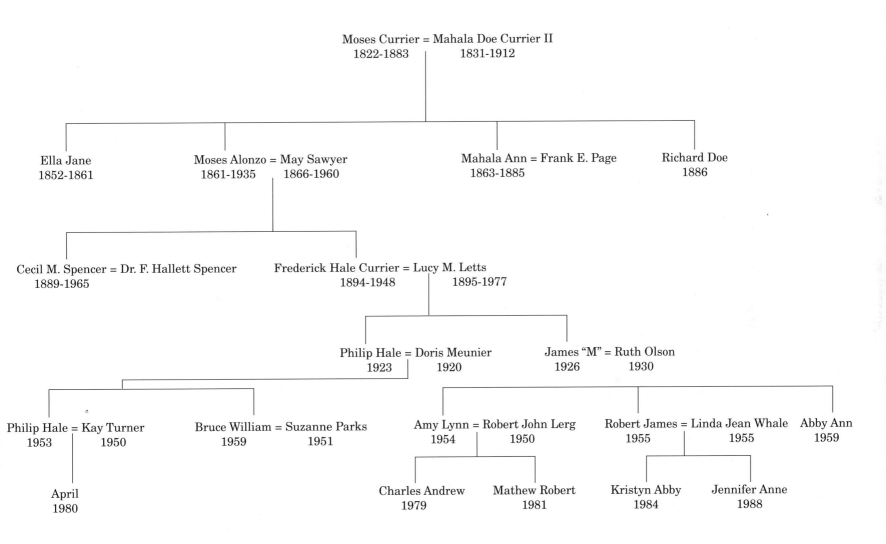

Moses Currier = Mahala Doe Currier II
1822-1883   1831-1912

Ella Jane
1852-1861

Moses Alonzo = May Sawyer
1861-1935   1866-1960

Mahala Ann = Frank E. Page
1863-1885

Richard Doe
1886

Cecil M. Spencer = Dr. F. Hallett Spencer
1889-1965

Frederick Hale Currier = Lucy M. Letts
1894-1948   1895-1977

Philip Hale = Doris Meunier
1923   1920

James "M" = Ruth Olson
1926   1930

Philip Hale = Kay Turner
1953   1950

Bruce William = Suzanne Parks
1959   1951

Amy Lynn = Robert John Lerg
1954   1950

Robert James = Linda Jean Whale
1955   1955

Abby Ann
1959

April
1980

Charles Andrew
1979

Mathew Robert
1981

Kristyn Abby
1984

Jennifer Anne
1988

=   Married

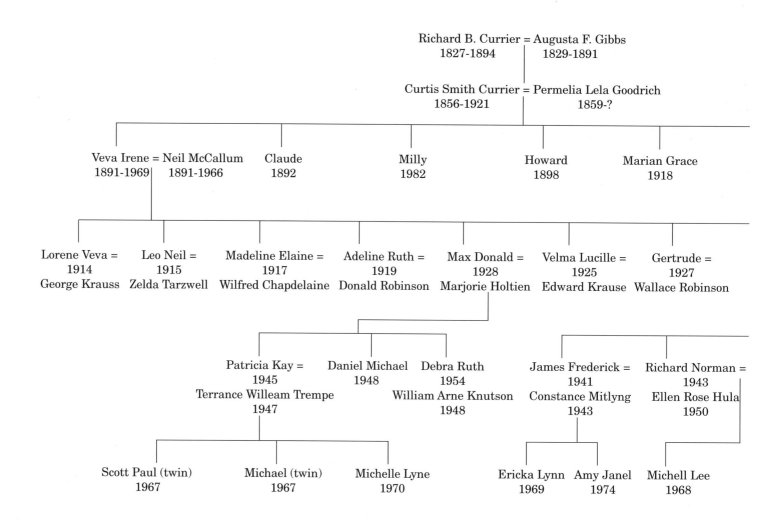

49. Richard B. Currier genealogy chart
In this line, the second youngest brother out of six brothers lived to be 67 years old and had only one son, Curtis Smith Currier. However, Richard Currier's family has produced more people living and dead in modern times than the descendants of his brothers and is the only line to produce male Curriers in the modern generation. The total number of descendants of Richard Currier is 44.

= Married

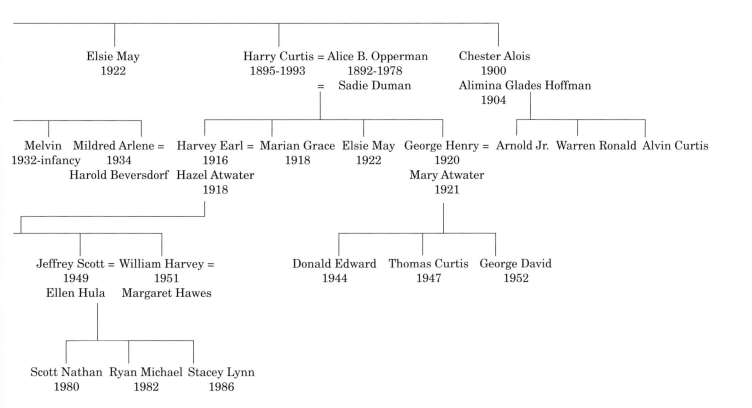

Elsie May
1922

Harry Curtis = Alice B. Opperman
1895-1993   1892-1978
        =   Sadie Duman

Chester Alois
1900
Alimina Glades Hoffman
1904

Melvin   Mildred Arlene =   Harvey Earl = Marian Grace   Elsie May   George Henry =   Arnold Jr.   Warren Ronald   Alvin Curtis
1932-infancy   1934   1916   1918   1922   1920
              Harold Beversdorf   Hazel Atwater   Mary Atwater
                                      1918   1921

Jeffrey Scott = William Harvey =
    1949   1951
  Ellen Hula   Margaret Hawes

Donald Edward   Thomas Curtis   George David
    1944   1947   1952

Scott Nathan   Ryan Michael   Stacey Lynn
    1980   1982   1986

CHAPTER SEVEN

The Modern Restoration

Restoration of the Currier octagon provides more than a fascinating focus for the story of a family and a community. Its survival also enables us to relish the wellsprings of creativity that helped to build a great state.

The unique octagon remained in Currier family ownership until the death of Mary Currier, wife of Moses Alonzo Currier, in 1960.[1] She was 91 and bequeathed the house to two grandsons, Philip and James, both of whom have fond memories of visiting their grandmother at the octagon when they were young. By 1961, however, both were well established in their careers, James as a dentist and Philip as a key executive with the State Liquor Control Commission. Their homes were located a significant distance from Almont, making it impossible for them to take care of the house.

Reluctantly, they sold it to William and Mary Hahn

49. The Restoration Team
(from left to right) Robert Glavich, his son, Sean Glavich, Kenneth Wright and Larry Johnston sitting on the front steps of the house.

for $5,000. For the first time in more than 100 years the octagon was occupied by non-Curriers, but Philip and James felt it was in good hands. The Hahns cherished the design and handled the house with care. In a 1983 newspaper interview, Hahn said, "I always told my friends you couldn't beat this octagon design for building a good, sound family home with tasteful richness."[2]

The Hahns' attentiveness was evident in their painstaking yet minor alterations, most of which were made over a period of six years before the family moved in. Mary carefully removed coats of paint from the woodwork and paneling and as many as five layers of wallpaper which she replaced with carefully selected designs in keeping with the original construction period. She then decorated the home with her family antiques and conscientiously refinished a portrait of Deacon F.P. Currier which had been left in an oval wood frame.

While Mary busily worked the interior, William, owner of Hahn Heating and Plumbing in Almont, used his skills to modernize both systems in the house. He installed a bathroom where the large pantry west of the kitchen had been located and provided a dual heating system, allowing him to heat only the first floor if he so desired. He also tore down the partition wall between the rear shed and the kitchen and the carriage house.[3] Philip remembers his grandfather, Moses Alonzo, chopping wood in that room to fuel the kitchen's cast iron stove.

Hahn made one significant alteration which must sadden the Curriers and passersby who remember the old lilac tree. Approximately the age of the house, the tree had reached a diameter of 10 to 14 inches and draped the driveway with its blossoms and sweet ambrosia. Hahn probably removed it because its roots were disturbing the foundation.

Overall, alterations made by the Hahns did not compromise the integrity of the octagon since they carefully analyzed any changes before they were implemented. Mrs. Hahn was unable to fully enjoy the fruits of her labors; she died in the house on March 26, 1974, one year before it was listed in the National Register of Historic Places. Mr. Hahn continued to live there until his death in 1985. He bequeathed the house and adjacent acreage to the Almont Hospital.

Our story now comes full circle because Frederick P. Currier IV, great grandson of the man who built it, purchased the octagon in April 1985, saying he wanted "to restore the house the way it was when my great grandfather had it. I want the octagon house to really look sparkling, and help Almont," and he approached the restoration with the necessary love, care and enthusiasm.

Actual work was patiently undertaken by carpenters from Larry Johnston's company and Ken Wright. The Robert Glaviches (he is a high school teacher and coach) took on the responsibility for the finishing work: stripping floors, painting, plaster work and wallpapering.

Stabilization of the roof was done first since water leakage had already damaged the interior. Next to be given attention were the western and eastern sections of the porch. Currier fortunately possessed several photographs from the late 19th century and used them as guides in restoring the house and porch. A wrought iron fence that at one time adorned the front of the house, which also featured a wood sidewalk, will be reproduced. The regular-coursed cobblestone foundation was stabilized, retaining its original appearance which is clearly visible on the west wall.

Restoration of the porch and its columns was a long and arduous task, costing about $10,000. Twelve octagonal porch posts necessitated accurate matching and milling of new ones. The rotting porch floor, front and side porch steps and porch apron latticework were replaced with Wolmanized lumber.[4]

Orson Fowler would have been pleased with our modern-day method of energy efficiency. Insulation was blown into the octagonal walls, and storm windows were replaced to maximize heat containment in the cold Michigan winters. The garage, rear storage room and room above the garage were insulated in 1988.

All floors with linoleum were stripped down to the hard wood. Interestingly, some of the floors had been painted only four or five inches away from the wall, indicating the use of large throw rugs. Stripping the kitchen floor also revealed holes where water had been pumped up from the cistern in the basement for cooking and washing purposes. The kitchen was remodeled with modern plumbing fixtures, wall cabinets for food and dish storage, and installation of a dishwasher and microwave oven. Original molding strips with square cut nails have been retained in the kitchen.

Four to five layers of wallpaper in rooms not restored by the Hahns were removed by the Glaviches, disclosing holes where stove pipes carried smoke out of the house through chimney flues. As many as five were discovered on the north wall of the kitchen. New wallpaper was selected by Currier following designs popular in the late 19th century. The second floor bedroom walls were replaced and wallpapered by the Glaviches, and a false window was installed between two southern octagon rooms. Lighting and heating elements were replaced throughout the house.

Despite being occupied since it was built in about 1854, the Currier Octagon has survived with only a few modernizing alterations and dramatically reflects a unique application of Orson Fowler's principles and the innovative character of its builder, Frederick Plumer Currier. It will endure as a monument to him to be enjoyed by future Almont generations, Currier family members, students of history and architecture, and curious visitors who most certainly will be fascinated by stories of the lives of its former occupants. Truly they were pioneers in the history of a great state.

Footnotes

1. At the time of her death, Mary Currier was living in Waverly, N. Y. with her daughter, Cecil Spencer. She had moved there in 1958. Mark Harmon, a boarder of the house for several years, was occupant and caretaker of the octagon after she left.

2. Marianne Jordan, "Almont Home Restoration in his Labor of Love," *Tri-City Times* (March 9,1983), 1.

3. This room originally was used as a woodshed and later as a storage area.

4. Wolmanized lumber is a wood chemically treated to extend its life. This process replaces the outdated use of creosote.

BIBLIOGRAPHY

Alma High School Yearbook, 1911. Published by the Class of 1911.

Beers, F.W. & Co., *Atlas of Lapeer County, Michigan, from Recent and Actual Surveys and Records under the Superintendence of F.W. Beers 1874,* (Published by F.W. Beers & Co., N.Y. Printed by Charles Hart, engraved by I.E. Neuman, 36 Vestry St., N.Y.)

Bond, Virginia, Joyce Rapes and Katherine Bliss, *History of the Washington Octagon House,* February 11, 1952.

Bowman, Hildamae Waltz, *Almont, The Tale of Then and Now,* (1985, no publishing information).

Boyum, Burton H., "Burt's Solar Compass," (Published in Historical Notes Number One,*Frank G. Matthews Sr., Memorial Fund.* May 1987.)

Bradford, T.B., *1838 Map of Michigan, including counties surveyed to that date,* (Michigan Historical Collections, Bentley Historical Library, The University of Michigan).

Brown, Alan S., "William Austin Burt—A Pioneer Michigan Inventor," *Michigan Heritage,* (Spring 1963, Vol. 4, No. 3, The Kalamazoo Valley Genealogical Society, Kalamazoo, Michigan) 149–153.

Creese, Walter, "Fowler and the Domestic Octagon," *Art Bulletin,* (June 1946, Volume 28) 89–102.

Currier, H.A. & Bro., Almont, Michigan, Manufacturers *Illustrated Catalogue of Farm Tools* (McCormack, Printer, Detroit ca. 1880).

Currier, Philip, Descendant of Moses Currier Jr., Oral communication, November 1988.

Dunham, F.A. Chief Engineer, *Atlas and Directory of Lapeer County, Michigan,* (Made for Actual Surveys and Officials Records, 1893, published by the Lapeer County Atlas Co., F.J. Hubbard in charge of field work, E. Robinson Co., Engravers and Printers, N.Y.)

Ellis, J. Dee, *Pioneer Families and History of Lapeer County, Michigan,* (Ellis Publishing Co., 3034 W. Oregon Rd., Lapeer, Michigan, 48440, 1978).

Eubanks, Sarah Ward, *National Register Nomination, West Saint Clair Historic District* 1986, (Listed in the National Register of Historic Places).

Finfer, Lawrence, *National Register Nomination, Currier Octagon, April 25, 1975,* (Listed in the National Register of Historic Places).

Fowler, Orson S., *The Octagon House, A Home For All,* (Dover Publications, Inc., New York, N.Y., 1973, a republication of work originally published in 1853 by Fowler and Wells under the title *A Home For All, or The Gravel Wall and Octagon Mode of Building.* First edition in 1848 was *A Home For All or a New, Cheap, Convenient, and Superior Mode of Building.*)

Geil, Samuel, *Map of Lapeer, Michigan from Special Surveys and Records, 1863,* (Published by Samuel Geil, Philadelphia, W.E. Doughty and I. Gross, chief Engineers under Superintendence of Geil and Harly), Michigan Historical Collections, Bentley Historical Library, The University of Michigan.

Glavich, Robert, director of the octagon restoration, 1987–1989, oral interview, October 1988.

Hoyt, David W., *The Old Families of Salisbury and Amesbury, Massachusetts*, (Providence, Rhode Island, 1898).

Jordan, Marianne, "Almont Home Restoration is His Labor of Love," (*Tri-City Times*, March 9, 1983).

Property Abstracts 1842, 1849, 1850, 1851, 1852, 1854, 1858, Lapeer County Record of Deeds, Liber 1, 1835–1858, Lapeer County Courthouse, Lapeer, Michigan.

The Macomb Daily, "Octagon House as Alive Now at It Was In 1860", February 25, 1976, Section 4B.

Massey James C. and Shirley Maxwell, "Octagons and Hexagons and Other Multi-Faceted Eccentricities," *Old House Journal*, June 1986.

McAlester, Virginia and Lee, *A Field Guide to American Houses*, (Alfred A. Knopf, Inc., New York, N.Y., 1984).

MAP, DRAWING AND PHOTOGRAPHY CREDITS

Page, H.R., *History of Lapeer County, Michigan with Illustrations and Biographical Sketches of Some of its Prominent Men and Pioneers*, (H.R. Page & Co., Chicago, Ill., 1884).

Schmidt, Carl F. & Philip Parr, *More About Octagons*, (No publishing date or information).

Schweitzer, Robert A., "Octagon Houses", *Chronicle, The Quarterly Magazine of the Historical Society of Michigan*, Winter 1981, 16-19.

Letters of Horatio Shaw to his brother and sister, 1845-1848. Michigan Historical Collections, Bentley Historical Library, The University of Michigan.

Sloane, Eric, *Our Vanishing Landscape,* (Random House, Inc., New York, N.Y., 1955).

Souvenir of Yale, Michigan, 1903, (Published by *The Record*, illustrated by Will Bailes).

Stuart, Donna Valley and Peter Schmitt76 76, "Octagons", *Michigan in Books,* Summer, 1973, Vol. 12, No. 3, 5-8.

United States Bureau of Census, 1850, 1860, Products of Industry, Lapeer County, (Michigan Historical Collections, Bentley Historical Library, The University of Michigan).

Veness, Nellie, "Almont, Michigan", *Flint Genealogical Quarterly*, October, 1967, Vol. 9, No. 4, 88-89.

a. Front view of the Currier Octagon
Robert Hensleigh

b. Boot scraper
Robert Hensleigh

c. Back view or ceiling
Robert Hensleigh

1. 19th century map of Almont, 1835
Anonymous

2. Frederick P. Currier I
Anonymous

3. Engraving of Currier Octagon
Anonymous

4. Henry Curryer genealogy chart
F.P. Currier IV and T. Cacciola

5. Frederick Plumer Currier I genealogy chart
F.P. Currier IV and T. Cacciola

6. Early Almont Township map
Beer's Atlas, 1893

7. Stump puller with man
Lewis Fitch

8. Stump fence
Lewis Fitch

9. Currier Octagon c. 1890
Anonymous

10. Early street map of Almont
F.A. Dunham Atlas, 1893

11. The Andrus Octagon
Robert Hensleigh

12. The Burt Octagon
Robert Hensleigh

13. First floor architectural drawing
Jeffrey Winstel

14. The Currier Octagon cellar
Robert Hensleigh

15. Currier Octagon porch window
Robert Hensleigh

16. Currier Octagon foyer
Robert Hensleigh

17. Detail of post
Robert Hensleigh

18. Second floor architectural drawing
Jeffrey Winstel

19. Belvedere cupola
Robert Hensleigh

20. Detail of Currier Octagon ceiling molding
Robert Hensleigh

21. Detail of Currier Octagon wainscoting
Robert Hensleigh

22. Architectural drawing of Belvedere
Jeffrey Winstel

23. Architectural drawing of Currier Octagon cellar
Jeffrey Winstel

24. Agricultural Works
Anonymous

25. Machine shop workers
Anonymous

26. Currier Plow No. 1
Copy Print by Robert Hensleigh

27. Currier Plow No. 2
Copy Print by Robert Hensleigh

28. Currier and Bros. farm tool catalogue
Copy Print by Robert Hensleigh

29. Graham Terry house
F. P. Currier IV

INDEX